Adopted by Indians

Related Titles from Heyday Books

Adopted by

INDIANS

A True Story

Thomas Jefferson Mayfield

Edited by
Malcolm Margolin

Illustrations by
Hilair Chism
Rick Jones

Heyday Books
Berkeley, California

Publisher's Cataloging-in-Publication
(Provided by Quality Books, Inc.)

Mayfield, Thomas Jefferson, ca. 1843-1928
     Adopted by Indians: a true story / Thomas Jefferson Mayfield ;
     edited by Malcolm Margolin ; illustrations by Hilair Chism, Rick
     Jones. -- 1st ed.
     p. cm.
     SUMMARY: A children's version of Indian summer : traditional life
     among the Choinumne Indians of California's San Joaquin Valley, a
     biography of Thomas Jefferson Mayfield.
     ISBN: 0-930588-93-2

     1. Mayfield, Thomas Jefferson, ca. 1843-1928--Juvenile
literature. 2. Yokuts Indians--Social life and customs--Juvenile
literature. 3. California--History--1850-1950--Juvenile literature.
I. Mayfield, Thomas Jefferson, ca. 1843-1928. Indian summer. II.
Title.

E99.Y75M39 1997   979.4'004974
                                         QB197-40817

Cover design: Jack Myers, DesignSite, Berkeley, CA.
Cover image: Rick Jones, Corvallis, OR.
Interior Design and Typesetting: Laura Harger and Rebecca LeGates,
based on original design by Jeannine Gendar, Berkeley, CA.
Printed by Transcontinental Printing, Inc., Canada.

The publishers wish also to express gratitude to Mona Latta Olsen for permission to use material previously published by her father, Frank Latta.

Please address orders, inquiries, and correspondence to:
Heyday Books
P.O. Box 9145, Berkeley, CA 94709
Phone (510) 549-3564; Fax (510) 549-1889
heyday@heydaybooks.com

Printed in Canada
10 9 8 7 6 5 4 3 2 1

Table of Contents

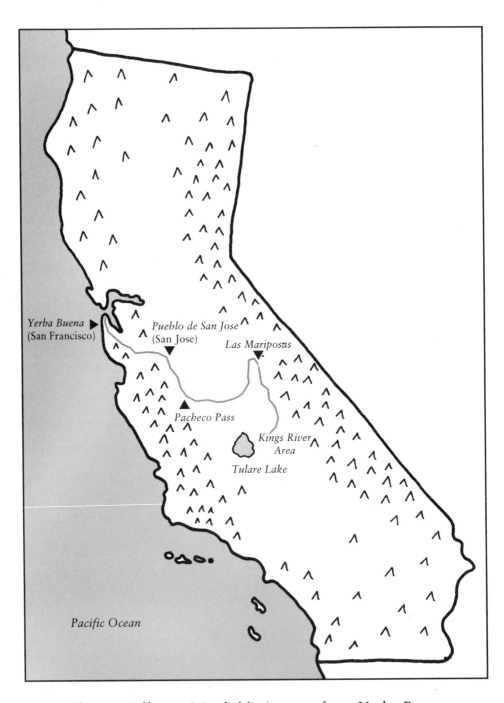

Thomas Jefferson Mayfield's journey from Yerba Buena
to the San Joaquin Valley

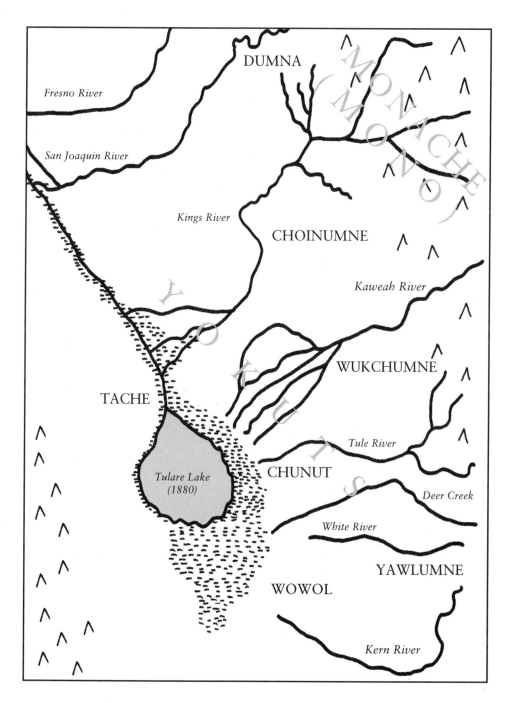

Indian groups of the Southern San Joaquin Valley

Introduction

t is a warm spring day in 1928. A very old man, seated on the front porch of a small store in White River, California, begins to spin a fascinating tale. He tells of a broad, beautiful valley where herds of elk and antelope once roamed free, where fish swarmed the rivers, and millions of birds filled the air. He tells of the Indian people who lived in prosperous villages along the shores of rushing rivers and quiet lakes. Then, lowering his voice, he tells of the small white boy who hunted and fished, played and slept alongside the Indians.

The old man was Thomas Jefferson Mayfield. He was talking to a much younger man, Frank Latta, a school teacher and historian who had come to interview him about his life.

And what an unusual life it was!

In 1850, when Mayfield was eight years old, he was adopted by the Choinumne Indians of California. Although his own family was white, young Thomas lived for the next ten years just like a Choinumne child, spending a happy and adventurous youth among native people who were still following their traditional ways.

The Choinumne Indians lived in what is now called the San Joaquin Valley. The San Joaquin Valley is huge, 65 miles across and 270 miles long. It spreads out between two steep mountain ranges, the Sierra to the east and the Coast Range to the west. Many rivers flow from the Sierra Mountains into this valley. In the old days, as the mountain snows melted, these rivers would swell, overflowing their banks each spring to form vast marshes and shallow lakes.

About eighty thousand people lived in this amazing valley and in the surrounding foothills. They belonged to many different "tribes." In addition to the Choinumne, there were the Tache, Wowol, Chunut, Yawlumne, Wukchumne, and many others. Each tribe was a small nation: it had its own territory, its own leaders, its own beliefs and customs. Each tribe spoke a distinct dialect of a language called Yokuts. Other Indians, who spoke entirely different languages, lived around them. Among these other groups were the Mono, or Monache as they are called in this book, who lived in the Sierra mountains, east of the valley.

Indian people had been living in the San Joaquin Valley for many thousands of years. Game, fish, and plant foods were plentiful, and people prospered. But once California became part of the United States, times became very hard for Indian people. Tens of thousands of newcomers flocked to California when gold was discovered in 1848. In their eagerness for wealth, they dirtied the rivers where the Indians used to fish. When the gold ran out, many of the settlers turned to farming and ranching. They simply took the land where Indians had been living. Soon, soldiers began to push the Indians onto reservations. Many Indians died. Only a few years after Thomas Mayfield's happy childhood with the Choinumne, many of the traditional ways of Indian life disappeared from the San Joaquin Valley.

After he became an adult, Thomas Jefferson Mayfield held many jobs. He mined for gold in the desert and herded sheep in the mountains. He lived to be an old man. But for most of his life, Mayfield did not talk about his childhood among the Indians. He feared that white listeners would not understand how he felt and would make fun of him. Only in the last days of his life did he tell this wonderful story to the young schoolteacher, Frank Latta. Latta kept coming back to interview the elderly Mayfield until he felt he had recorded the whole story. Only a few hours later, Thomas Jefferson Mayfield died. The story he left behind is completely true, and it is very beautiful. We are lucky to have it.

The Choinumne Indians no longer live in their old villages or follow many of their traditional ways. But they are very much alive. Just the other day I met a young Choinumne woman who is learning the Choinumne language from one of the older people who still speaks it. She is very pleased to be learning this beautiful language, and she is very proud to be a Choinumne Indian. As you read this book, I hope you will understand why she is so proud.

Malcolm Margolin
Berkeley, California

Adopted by Indians

Chapter One

Searching for Gold

MY DADDY WAS born in Kentucky. His folks had a large plantation and a great many slaves and racehorses. They were quite wealthy and my daddy traveled a great deal when he was young.

When my daddy was about eighteen, a man by the name of Andrew Jackson was having some trouble with a lot of Englishmen. He needed help, and so my daddy went with him to a place called New Orleans. There, in the swamps, they had a battle with the Englishmen and ran them out into the water. This was called the War of 1812. My daddy always said that this man Jackson was a real fighter. Jackson liked my daddy, too, and made him a lieutenant.

While my daddy was with Jackson, he met some men who had been to a place away out west, and they told him so many stories about this place that after a few years he went out there. There he met a man named Sam Houston. This man Houston was having trouble with some Mexicans. My daddy went with him, and Houston made my daddy a captain, and he made himself president of a country he called Texas.

In Brazos County, Texas, my daddy met and married a Miss Maria Curd. There were three children born to them: John Mayfield, about 1826; Ben Mayfield, about 1831; and Thomas Jefferson Mayfield, myself, about 1843.

While my daddy was with Houston he thought he would quit fighting and settle down, but this man Houston turned Texas over to the United States. After fighting again, this time in Mexico, my daddy decided to take the family to California and look for gold.

We started to California along a road they called the Santa Fe Trail. After we had gone a long way, we received news that Indians called Mescalero Apaches had killed some of the people with a wagon train ahead of us. We returned to Galveston, Texas, and waited for a ship to San Francisco, which we then called Yerba Buena.

We were six months and a few days on the water. Practically every day of this time was spent in the midst of a raging storm. We were blown around Cape Horn, at the tip of South America, completely out of control and expecting to go on the rocks at any moment. However, we were blown around the rocks and into clear water on the Pacific side. During this rounding of the horn there were only three men who weren't sick and were able to go on deck, and they were helpless in the storm.

On the trip up the Pacific, conditions were just as bad. We were blown hundreds of miles out to sea, and were four weeks in getting back on our course. When we arrived in Yerba Buena there were only three able-bodied men to bring the ship into port.

Of this trip I distinctly remember being cooped up between decks for what seemed to me years, and also occasional glimpses of mountainous waves. I also remember my mother holding me close to her together with my older brother, Ben, when we were in particularly dangerous places.

There are only one or two things about the landing at Yerba Buena that I remember clearly. We anchored among a sea of idle ships and at what seems to have been a great distance from shore. Our small boat, which carried the passengers ashore, landed to the south of a considerable marsh. There was a small wooden wharf where our boat landed, and a large, slimy mudflat. I remember seeing stoves that had apparently been dumped off in the mud.

The landing at Yerba Buena (San Francisco)

Of Yerba Buena I remember very little. We were all in a hurry to get to the mines. As I recollect, there were several adobe buildings and a cluster of tents and wooden frames with canvas or some sort of white cloth tacked over them. The place was hilly and covered with brush and scrub oak. It was not a large place, and the buildings I have mentioned were set on the hills in the brush without any attempt at building real streets. Near the water the roadways were seas of mud.

We spent only a few days in Yerba Buena. My daddy was going to the Fremont Mines at Las Mariposas in the Sierra foothills. So he bought three pack animals and four saddle horses with equipment, and we started out. Leaving Yerba Buena, we traveled south toward Pueblo de San Jose [the town now called San Jose]. The first night we camped at a small stream.

I remember that a number of the long-horned cattle so familiar to us in Texas came along. Just before dark an Indian *vaquero* [cowboy] rode by and drove the cattle toward the east. This *vaquero* was a very interesting person and rode a fine horse. He was quite dark and straight and rode as though he was a part of the horse.

The Indian dismounted and talked to my daddy in Spanish. He said that he was riding for a Spaniard who lived nearby. We all

crowded close to look at his silver-mounted bridle and spurs, and we watched him drive the cattle away.

The next day about noon we arrived at Pueblo de San Jose. We stopped long enough to lay in our last supplies, as my daddy did not expect to be able to buy anything more until we reached the mines.

In my memory I have only a picture of San Jose as a quiet, sleepy village. The row of adobe buildings where we stopped formed one side of a large, open square. I did not want to dismount, as there were a number of large, hungry-looking dogs growling and sniffing about, and there were tough-looking men sitting on a bench against the wall in front of the store where we were stopped. My daddy said they would be a hard lot to meet after dark.

The second night we spent at John Gilroy's ranch. During the night we were bothered by cattle. They made quite a fuss and we were watchful for fear they would run over us. We drove them away several times, but in the morning they were standing a short distance away in a circle about our camp.

Adobe buildings

Leaving Gilroy's ranch early in the morning, we followed a trail that led away to the southeast. This trail was to lead us to Pacheco Pass, which was the best route into the San Joaquin Valley south of Livermore's Pass. The way went through very low foothills to a broad, gravelly creek bottom covered with sycamores. There we camped for the night close to the creek, which was a fresh, clear stream about thirty feet wide and a foot or more in depth.

It was long before sunup when we started up the creek toward the pass.

Chapter Two

The Finest Country We Have Ever Seen

AFTER WE HAD almost reached the summit of the pass, I begged to be allowed to ride on one of the pack animals. I had been riding on a folded blanket behind my mother's saddle, and from there could not see ahead. She did not like to have me ride the pack animals, as they might have brushed me off when they passed under low branches. But as the country grew more level and we came to a large, flat meadow, she had my oldest brother place me on top of one of the packs.

I remember that there were five or six deer feeding in the meadow and that they did not run away, but watched us closely as we passed at a distance of about two hundred yards.

As we left the meadow and again entered the woods to the east, my daddy and brother Ben were riding ahead. Then came the three pack animals, mine being the third. Brother John came behind me, driving the loose animals. Then came Mother, the last of the procession, interested in the new valley we were about to enter, but watching me most of the time. I remember that I proudly smiled back at her from my perch on the pack ahead, and that she returned my smile.

Suddenly my daddy pointed over the tops of the bare hills ahead of us and exclaimed, "Look there!" And there in the distance, until then lost to us in the haze, was our valley. A shining thread of light marked El Rio de San Joaquin [the San Joaquin River], flowing, as my mother said, "through a crazy quilt of color."

How excited we all were. Everyone wanted to talk at once. Then someone noticed, still farther to the east, that what we had at first taken for clouds was a high range of snow-covered peaks, their bases lost in the purple haze.

Finally we started on and passed down the long ridge, which my daddy called a "hog's back," to the small valley below. There we found that the grass we had seen from above was wild oats. They stood as high as our stirrups and were as thick as they could grow. My daddy said that was the finest country he had ever seen.

Under a grove of large cottonwoods and sycamores, we found the buildings of El Rancho de San Luis. Here we were made welcome by a pretty native Californian, who talked Spanish to us and took my mother and me inside with her.

The inside of the building was of interest to me, as I had not been in one just like it before. There was an earthen floor which had been smoothed and beaten hard. In one corner was a raised adobe plat-form. There the cooking was done. In the opposite corner was a crude bed made of a cowhide stretched over a rough wooden frame.

There were two chairs in the room, and a few garments hanging on the wall.

After a short visit we made camp under a large cottonwood tree on the bank of the creek a few yards northeast of the building. Here there was a large, deep pool of water. I have always remembered that place as one of the most ideal I have ever seen. The tall, green grass, the cool, clear water, and the trees with their fresh leaves made as pretty a spot as one could wish.

We left Rancho de San Luis early the next morning, before anyone was stirring at the adobe house. By this time we could see what had caused the mass of color so noticeable from the mountain the day before. The entire plain, as far as we could see, was covered with wildflowers. Almost all of the flowers were new to us.

Along the creek were many blue lupines, some of them growing on bushes six and eight feet high. The low foothills were covered with two pretty, lily-like flowers, one tall and straight-stemmed with a cluster of lavender, bell-shaped flowers at the top, and the other a purple, ball-shaped blossom on a similar stem.

As we passed below the hills, the whole plain was covered with great patches of rose, yellow, scarlet, orange, and blue. The colors did not seem to mix. Each kind of flower liked a certain kind of soil best and some of the patches of color were a mile or more across.

I believe that we were more excited out there on the plains among the wildflowers than we had been when we saw the valley for the first time from the mountain the day before. Several times we stopped to pick the different kinds of flowers, and soon we had our horses and packs decorated with masses of all colors.

My daddy had traveled a great deal, and it was not easy to get him excited about wildflowers or pretty scenery. But he said that he would not have believed that such a place existed if he had not seen it himself. And my mother cried with joy, and wanted to make a home right there in the midst of it all.

For my own part, I have never seen anything to equal the virgin San Joaquin Valley before there was a plow or a fence in it. I have always loved nature and have liked to live close to her. Many times, when I have traveled alone in later years and night has overtaken me, I have tied my horse and rolled up in my saddle blanket and slept under a bank or among the wildflowers or on the desert under a bush. I remember those experiences as the greatest in my life. The two most beautiful remembrances I have are of the virgin San Joaquin Valley and my mother.

Many times since, I have seen all of the things I saw on that first trip through the valley. But when I think of those things, I see them as I saw them from my perch on the pack horse. They were all new then, and strange, and they made an impression that has not faded in the seventy-eight years that have since passed. (I do not mean by this that I have ever been back to Pacheco Pass, or to San Jose, or to San Francisco, for I have never been over that trail since that spring day in 1850.)

There were great dens of ground squirrels. They had thrown the soil up in many places to a height of two feet or more over an area of thirty yards square. Over this area their burrows were thick, and they would stand and bark at us by the hundreds as we approached. When we came close they would disappear, but as soon as we had passed they would stand braver than ever and bark at us as long as we were in hearing.

In some places badgers had either thrown the earth up much as the squirrels had, or they had driven out the squirrels and had enlarged and taken over their burrows.

I also remember glimpses of great droves of antelope standing out against the horizon at a distance, but we did not see any of them at close range. We also saw, to our right, a band of rapidly moving animals. My daddy said that these were horses. They kept at a distance, but seemed to be watching and following us.

When we neared the San Joaquin River we saw about twenty elk. We had approached quite close to them, but did not see them at once, and they hurried away through a low swale, or dry slough, which paralleled the river. I will always remember how quickly they

A herd of elk

disappeared and how clever they were at making use of the cover. There were a few oak trees near, and the elk kept these between us and themselves. They lowered their heads with their horns against their necks and shoulders and sneaked along as rapidly as a horse could run.

We also saw some tracks along the river that my daddy said were made by bears. They must have been grizzlies, as I have found since that they were the only bears along the San Joaquin.

The most amusing sight I remember on the plains before we reached the San Joaquin River was a large flock of sandhill cranes. We passed within forty yards of some of them and they hardly noticed us. Quite a large group of them were holding a sort of meeting. They would all jabber a while and then they would do a sort of dance. We laughed at them for a long while; they were so sober and earnest about it.

The dance of sandhill cranes

We had been told at the Rancho de San Luis that there was a ferry about twenty-five miles north, where the Merced River emptied into the San Joaquin. They said that this ferry had only been running for a few months. But we had decided that a trip to the ferry would take us too far out of our way, and we intended to use the ford they had described.

As we approached the river we found the water quite high, and had some difficulty in reaching the river. We finally reached the bank over some high ground. The river was too high to ford. So my daddy unloaded the pack animals and made them swim across. Then my mother and brothers swam their horses across, taking my daddy's horse with them. He had tied all of our ropes together and they took one end of this long line across with them. Then my daddy made a raft of dead willow branches and ferried our supplies across. He accomplished this by tying one end of the long line to the raft. My brother John tied the other end to a tree on the east bank. Then he mounted the raft and poled it away from the bank. As it drifted downstream, the rope pulled it around to the east bank.

On the east side of the river we experienced a great deal more trouble than we had on the west. It took us several hours to find our way around and through the sloughs that extended many miles east of the San Joaquin River.

Great clouds of blackbirds arose as we passed, and we saw great growths of tule reeds. Those tules must have been twenty feet high and two or more inches in thickness. We were as completely lost in them as we would have been in a forest.

Chapter Three

Meeting the Indians

A FTER SEVERAL DAYS of plunging through tule reeds and mud and swimming and fording sloughs, we came out on a rolling, sloped country. Traveling eastward across this plain through the same wildflowers we had seen to the west, we finally encountered a trail, or what was really a wandering wagon road. Upon meeting several horsemen who were traveling along this road, we found that it led to the Fremont Mines, as Las Mariposas were then called. We traveled to our destination with the horsemen we had met.

My daddy was disappointed in the Fremont Mines. He had always lived in an unsettled country and at the mines he found a great crowd of miners racing around, buying and selling claims and doing some mining. Everything for miles around was staked. So he decided to move farther south.

At this time, there had been no rush of miners south of Las Mariposas, and we started south to the San Joaquin River where it flows westward from the Sierra. It was my daddy's plan to prospect that river for gold.

We arrived at the San Joaquin opposite an Indian *rancheria* [village]. Here the river bank was quite high and the water about one hundred yards across. A large group of Indians, numbering probably forty, were bathing in the south edge of the stream. As I remember, the group was composed mostly of young people. They all appeared very much excited at seeing our party, but did not seem afraid of us.

We sat on our horses a while and watched the bathers. Some of them were washing their hair. They would lean over, allowing their long hair to fall forward into the water. Then they would comb it with their fingers.

They soon became too deeply interested in us to go on with their bathing, and several of them swam to our side of the river. By this time we had dismounted and were trying to decide whether to attempt a crossing there, or to follow the north bank of the river toward the hills.

My daddy found that one of the Indians could understand a little Spanish, and this Indian encouraged him to cross the river, saying that his people would help us. So we made preparations to ferry the river, as we had done before when crossing the valley.

While the animals were being unpacked, I stayed near my mother, and she kept close watch over me, as eight or ten of the Indians were crowding about looking at me, excitedly talking to one another.

Finally a young girl about sixteen years of age offered to take me on her back and swim the river with me. At this my mother took me in her arms and held me close to her, motioning for the Indians to go away. She called to my daddy, and he ran to us, thinking that some hostile move had been made. He soon saw that the Indians were all right and told my mother to let the girl carry me across, as I would be safer with her than I would on one of our horses.

So my mother took off my clothes and put me on the back of the Indian girl. I clasped my hands around her neck, and she took my feet under her arms and waded into the water. Soon she started swimming with a long, overhand stroke. She was as slippery as could be, and I was afraid of being carried away by the current and clung to her neck so closely that she could not breathe. Several times she stopped swimming and reached up and pulled my arms down until she recovered her breath. Then she started on again, until we arrived at the south edge of the stream in shallow water. She stood me in the water, which was about a foot deep, near a sandbar. During this time all of the Indian women and children from the rancheria had accumulated where we were about to land, and they crowded around me and laughed and talked to each other about me and called me *"chólo wé-chep"* (little white boy). I did not know their language then, but I have always felt sure that they were also telling each other how cute I was.

The girl who had carried me across the river was very proud of me and, holding my hand, kept the rest of the Indians at a distance of several feet. She would talk to me and laugh, but of course I understood nothing she said, and remembered only the words I mentioned before.

After we had crossed the river, we spent several hours at the rancheria. Then we packed our animals again and traveled several miles upstream before we made camp. During the entire distance we were accompanied by a large group of Indians from the rancheria. After dark they left, but were back in the morning before sunrise with acorn bread and fresh meat for us.

The next day, after leaving the Indians, we proceeded up the river. There we found a couple of white men building a ferry. My daddy decided to stay there for a while and prospect the sand in the river. He soon found that there was some gold in it and built a long flume and sluice box of split logs in which to wash the sand.

During this time we were camped on a sandbar above the level of the river. About the time my daddy had his sluice box done, we had several days of real hot weather. It must have been about the first of July. There had been some discussion about high water, but we were not alarmed. I believe that the Indians had told us that there would be a flood. However, we made no preparations to move, as we felt that we were perfectly safe where we were.

The Indians still kept in touch with us, and brought us meat and bread. This we used almost entirely, as we did not have a large supply of our own, and it was a long trip to Stockton, the nearest large city, for more. They also made me a present of a fine bow and a half-dozen arrows.

One afternoon, while playing on the ferryboat with an Indian about my own age, I slipped and fell in the water. I could not swim and of course immediately went under. When I came up the Indian boy was lying on his stomach with the upper part of his body hang-

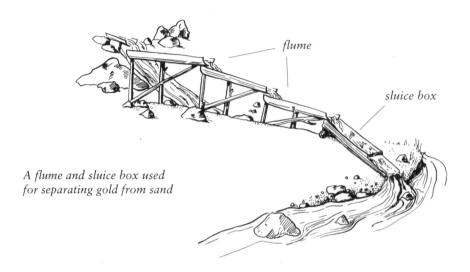

*A flume and sluice box used
for separating gold from sand*

ing over the edge of the boat. I would surely have drowned if it had
not been for him. He was not as big as I was, but he could swim like
a fish. He grabbed me by the hair and towed me around the edge of
the boat to shallow water where I could wade to shore. It was a
narrow escape, and I never forgot that Indian boy. I knew him for
many years afterward. His name was Koo-nance and he belonged to
the tribe [Dumna] that had a rancheria near where the town of
Millerton was later located.

One afternoon I had been shooting at a mark on the sandbar
below our camp with my bow and arrows. I left them out there
overnight. During the night we awakened and found several inches of
water within our tent. The river was rising rapidly and we rushed
about in the dark, working hard to save our supplies and equipment.
The thing that worried me most was my bow and arrows. I waded
around in the water looking for them, but was unable to find them,
as they had been carried away before our tent was flooded. While I
was looking for them, the folks missed me and began a search for

me. I soon appeared and they were glad to see me, but made me stay with our pile of equipment high up on the riverbank.

The next morning we were a discouraged family. We had lost part of our supplies, and the flume and sluice box were entirely gone. No one had known anything about conditions on the river except the Indians, and no one had paid any attention to what they said. We camped on the bank of the river for several days. The water rose high above where we had been camped on the sandbar. During this time we learned from the Indians that the river would be much as it was then until late in the summer. By this time about twenty Americans had gathered about the ferry and were prospecting the surrounding country.

After much discussion my daddy decided that he would move further south and make a permanent settlement on Kings River. He had been over there a few weeks previous to our being flooded out and liked the country on Kings River very much. He said he'd had enough of mining.

Mining equipment

My daddy wanted to raise horses and cattle. He decided that a foothill location would place him close to the free valley feed [grazing] during the spring, and also the later mountain feed during the summer. I believe that this was the same reason that many of the first settlers in the valley selected foothill locations. In many places the valley plains furnished free grazing until the late 1870s.

So we packed up and traveled south again until we arrived at the north bank of Kings River. We followed the north bank to the first good-sized stream flowing into it from the north. There, on the point of land formed by Kings River on the south and Sycamore Creek on the east, we again made camp.

There were many fine oak trees nearby. Sycamore Creek contained plenty of water and fish, and we felt sure that it would have running water in it all summer. If the water in Sycamore Creek should fail, then we would have Kings River nearby.

My daddy and my brothers, John and Ben, felled a tall oak tree and split it into shakes [shingles]. From these shakes they built a two-room shanty. The roof and sides were entirely of shakes. They also built a large stone fireplace. We now had a real home.

Chapter Four

Adopted by Indians

HEN WE FIRST came to Kings River, we met quite a number of Indians. They were of the same open-hearted, friendly disposition as those we had met on the San Joaquin.

On the south bank of Kings River, about opposite the mouth of Sycamore Creek, there was an Indian rancheria. There was another about a mile or two upstream from the first one. These were the people we knew best, and we soon came to know them well and to trust them completely.

During the first three years we were on Sycamore Creek, the Indians furnished most of our food. At first we used to hunt and fish a great deal, but we gradually quit it because they used to leave game hanging in the large oak tree in front of the house, and also left their acorn bread at the back door. Most of the time we would never see them do this, as they would bring the things while we were gone, or at night while we were asleep. We appreciated this a great deal, as it was a long, hard trip to Stockton after supplies, and we also had very little cash to spend. Several years later I learned from the Indians that they kept us in meat in order to keep us from firing our guns and scaring the game. Of course, we were always good to the Indians and gave them green corn and wheat, but we never in any way came near repaying them for what they did for us.

We made a very great distinction between the mountain Indians, or Monaches, and the valley Indians [Choinumne]. Our neighbors at the rancherias belonged to the valley group.

On Sycamore Creek we were at about the upstream limits of the valley Indians and the downstream limits of the Monaches. They both seemed to travel over it at will, but I believe it was used more by the valley group than by the Monaches.

The valley Indians would not mix with the mountain Indians. They did not talk the same dialect and the valley Indians considered themselves very much better than the Monaches. When members of the two groups would meet on a trail they would ignore each other. Some trading was carried on between the two groups, but I am sure it was done by a few members of each group who made a business of it and traveled back and forth between the groups.

Sometimes an Indian would come to the edge of the clearing at the back of the house and stand there for hours, looking in the back door and just watching what was going on. We were a whole lot more of a curiosity to them than they were to us, and when we were sure it was one of the valley Indians we paid no attention to him, as we knew that he was just curious to see how we did things. Of course, he would go back to the rancheria and, as I heard them do later when I was living with them, talk for hours to the rest of the Indians about what he had seen.

This reminds me how, when we first came to Kings River, the Indians used to go around after we had planted corn or potatoes and dig up the hills. They did not mean to do any damage. I believe that in many instances where the white settlers had trouble with the Indians it all started because the Indians were just curious to know what in the world the white settlers were doing, and not because they wanted to, or even knew, they were doing any damage.

One of the Indians made me a present of a fine sinew-backed bow of juniper and a half-dozen arrows. They called a bow *drah-lip* and an arrow *too-yosh*. This was really as nice a bow as they could get, and was painted in pretty colors. It was about three-and-one-half feet long and was made like they made their hunting bows, wide and flat and recurved at the ends, but pinched in or narrowed at the grip. It had been made by one of the Monaches and traded to the people who lived near us. (The Monaches did a lot of fighting and knew how to make good bows.) The string was made of sinew and secured at one end by wrapping it about the end of the bow. At the other end was a loop which would be slipped up into a nock [notch]. The string could be shortened by twisting or by adjusting it at the end opposite the nock.

The valley Indians could not make good bows, as they did not know how to make the waterproof glue with which to fasten the sinew to the back. They really had little use for a bow except for hunting, as they did no fighting among themselves, and there were so

many of them that the
mountain Indians very
seldom bothered them.
Then, too, most of their
game was caught with
snares and traps. They
made a crude sort of bow of
elderwood without backing and
without recurving at the ends. This
they used when they could not get the
Monache bows.

It is my belief that making bows, as well as
arrows and beads, was understood by only a few individuals, even
among the Monaches. I know that the Monaches used to take their
bows to a certain bowmaker in the mountains north of Sycamore
Creek to have him repair or replace the sinew backing on them. The
Monaches on Sycamore Creek and on Kings River, at least near us,
did not know how to do it. I know, too, that the Indians passed
down most of their arts from father to son and guarded their knowledge closely.

While my folks would have nothing to do with the Monaches, I
knew several of them quite well. A few of them could talk the dialect
of the valley Indians and I used to talk to them when I met them.
They were really better than we thought. By talking to them I came
to know many things about them that my folks did not know. I do
not believe that many of the other settlers on Kings River knew much
about them either.

Shortly after we settled on Kings River my mother died. It was a terrible blow to all of us. We never realized what she meant to us out there in the wilderness until after she had died. My daddy was gone a great deal of the time, running livestock in the valley and in the mountains. My brother John was riding part of the time for my daddy and part of the time for other settlers who had come to Kings River soon after we had. My brother Ben was old enough to go with either of them or to look out for himself. But I was younger, and I was quite a problem after Mother died.

The Indians at the rancheria had always taken an interest in me, and I had spent a great deal of time there before my mother died. She was always willing for me to go across the river with them, and I am sure she felt that I was perfectly safe with them.

Shortly after my mother died, the Indians at the rancheria held a meeting and decided to ask my daddy to let them take me and raise me. So they sent a delegation of five or six women over to our house to talk to my daddy. Of course he immediately said that he would never consent to any such thing. But after a long talk he decided to let me stay with them a few days while he was gone with his stock. When he returned I went back to him, but he was soon gone again. He was later gone so much that I was with the Indians almost continually.

I was with this tribe of Indians almost all of the time for nearly ten years. For at least two different periods of three years each I saw none of my own people. (This was not strictly true of the second three-year period, because I did see my daddy for about an hour

when he rode by one day while the Indians were at Tulare Lake. I will describe that meeting later, when I tell of our trips to the lake.)

While I was at the rancheria I came and went as I pleased. No one of the women claimed me. I was looked after by several of them. They treated me better than they did their own children and probably made a pretty badly spoiled boy of me. I was given the best of everything. They dressed me just as they did their own children while I was small. When I grew older I wore more clothing, generally a breechcloth like the older Indians.

Chapter Five

Talking "Indian"

ERY FEW of the Indians I lived with could talk any English. But before I went to live with them I had learned some of their language, and I very soon learned practically all of it.

To me the language of the valley Indians [the Choinumne] was always interesting. Compared with English, the Indian language I knew was throaty, a series of short syllables, but soft and musical. Many of their words were imitations of the sounds made by the things they represented. The word for squirrel was *skée-til*, and was spoken sharply, much as the squirrel barks. The word for the little ground owl, or billy-owl as we called it, was *péek-ook*, and the Indians bobbed their heads like he does when they said it. If you are close to the billy-owl when he bobs his head, you will hear him make a little sound like *péek-ook*. In some tribes the name for ground owl is *wá-tih-te*. Spoken shrilly and sharply, it is an imitation of the screeching call of the ground owl at twilight.

The word for hawk was *swoop*. The word for sleep was *wáwh-yen*, and it almost made me yawn to hear them say it.

The Choinumne name for the sun was *óo-push*. The moon they called *áw-push*. When the moon was getting smaller after it became full, they said that a bug was eating it, but that the bug always got too full before it ate the moon up and had to stop. Then the moon grew back to its full size again. During an eclipse they said that a coyote was eating the moon or sun. Then the medicine man used to put on his dance to overcome the coyote's power.

It was always interesting to me that the word *nim*, meaning "mine," was the exact reverse of *min*, meaning "yours." The word for "me" was *nah*, and for "you," *mah*. The word for both niece and nephew was *chi-úhk-nim*. If your meaning was not clear, you had to explain in your sentence just whom you meant.

Winter they called *taw-máw-kish*. Summer was *hi-él*. They did not use words for the other two seasons, spring and fall, that I know. The time when the wildflowers bloomed they called *tish-úm-yu*. I suppose it could be taken to mean spring.

In the spring the Indians were always gathering flowers and fastening them in their hair. If there was a patch of wildflowers anywhere near camp, you would see up to a couple of dozen people sitting in them or picking them. Baby-blue eyes were called *lúp-chen súh-suh,* or fish eyes. Chinese houses were *trá-el-le en-él-o*, or snake's dresses. Blue

Skée-til
(Squirrel)

lupines were *hói-up*, and the California poppy was *shuh-cúg-cuh*. There were dozens of others.

Sometimes the sharp tip of a fish gig [spear] would be broken off or become dull by striking the gravel in the bottom of the river when they were spearing fish. They called this *hóme-tun*, meaning blunt, or dull. But they could distinguish between a point that was dull and an edge that was dull. If the edge of an arrow point or a chipped stone knife became dull, they said it was *nih-súh-now*.

There is only one really hard sound to learn in the Choinumne language. It is a sort of an "h" made with a blowing sound, deep in the throat. When a white man tries to yell the letter "h" and blow through his throat at the same time, he loses all his breath before he makes any noise. But an Indian can yell a word with that sound in it so that you can hear it a good half-mile. I learned to do it just as well as the Indians.

The words for the four directions had several of these "h's" in them. *K-hú-sheem* was north. West was *t-hú-k-héel*. South was *k-hú-mote*. They often used these words when they were hunting for deer that had been wounded or killed. An Indian would stand on one side of a canyon and yell a half-mile to tell another Indian in which direction to look for a deer, and he would easily be heard.

Some sounds or endings mean the same that they do in other languages, but it is only an acci-

Hói-up
(Blue Lupine)

Trá-el-le en-él-lo
(Chinese houses)

Shuh-cúg-cuh
(California poppy)

Lúp-chen súh-suh
(Baby blue eyes)

dent that they do. I am always reminded of the Scotch word "wee," which we use in English to mean very small. In Indian, *wé-che* means very small. *Wé-ghe* is another word meaning small, but not so small as *wé-che*. *Wé-chet* means little sticks. *Wé-chep* means little child. You can almost always depend that the sound "wee" means something small. The only word I can think of that might be an exception is *we-há-set*, the name for mountain lion. And that might have to do with something about the animal that I do not know about.

When I had been with the Choinumne Indians for about six years, I could talk their language as well as most of the full-blood Indians. During this time I seldom talked anything but Indian. Most of it was very easy to learn. It was put together much like English. *He ahm* meant the same as "I am," "you are," "we are," "he is," "she is," or anything of the kind. *He ahm wih-níh-se* might mean "they are ready," "it is ready," "I am ready," "You are ready," or anything of the kind. If there was any chance for confusion, you had to explain by adding more to your sentence.

The Choinumne called the San Joaquin Valley *Chaw-láw-no*. *Wah-áh-hah bah-lú Chaw-láw-no* meant "away down the valley." If an Indian had been gone from the rancheria for an hour and you asked him where he had been, he might say, "*Wah tríp-in.*" That would mean that he had been up the river for a short walk. If he answered, "*Wah-áh-hah tríp-in,*" he would mean that he had gone quite a long distance. If he drew out a long "*Wah-áhhhhh-hah,*" stuck his lips out as far as he could, and pointed his mouth over the hills toward another valley, that would mean that he had been on the longest trip he had ever taken.

The word for father was *nó-pope* and for mother, *nó-um*. "Grand-mother" was *báh-pish*. "Sister" was *aw-gáwish* and "brother," *ná-bits*.

The Indians I lived with used the same system of counting that we do. Eleven was ten-one, twelve was ten-two, and so on to twenty. Twenty was two-ten, and twenty-one was two-ten-one. Of course they did not use our names for the numbers, but used the following:

one	*yá-et* (sounds almost like "yet")
two	*poó-noy*
three	*só-uh-pun*
four	*hóp-poo-noy*
five	*yách-chee-nil*
six	*chú-la-pee*
seven	*núm-chen*
eight	*moó-nosh*
nine	*só-pun-hut*
ten	*tréeo*
eleven	*treeo ya-et*
twelve	*treeo poo-noy*
thirteen	*treeo so-uh-pun*
twenty	*poo-noy treeo*
twenty-one	*poo-noy treeo ya-et*
twenty-two	*poo-noy treeo poo-noy*
thirty	*so-uh-pun treeo*
thirty-three	*so-uh-pun treeo so-uh-pun*
fifty	*yach-chee-nil treeo*
one hundred	*treeo treeo,* or ten tens. Or: *ya-et shinto*

The Indians could count into the millions and keep an absolutely accurate record of any number without writing of any kind. Although *treeo-treeo* meant one hundred, in counting they generally used the word *shinto*. *Ya-et shinto* meant one hundred, *poo-noy shinto* two hundred, and so on to *so-pun-hut shinto*, or nine hundred. One thousand was *ya-et tów-so* (the "ow" sounded as in "cow"). I know this word sounds like "thousand," and that it may be thought that they got it from the English language, but I am positive that it is not so.

I remember that I was on the shore of Tulare Lake with the Indians when a mile-long swarm of wild geese flew over. They actually darkened the sky. One of the old Indians looked up at them and said, *"Tow-so tow-so,"* which to us plainly meant a thousand thousands, or one million. This word was understood by all of the old Indians and I am sure was a part of their own language.

The Indian kept account of calculations without counters or marks in the sand. I rarely ever saw one count on his fingers. In this sort of calculation the average Indian was much better than the average white person.

I am sure that this system of counting was not gained from the Spanish, as the Indians had no knowledge of any other beside their own, and the real old Indians, with their noses pierced with a long piece of bone and their faces tattooed, used it. These old characters did not use any Spanish words, nor had they taken on any of the white man's customs.

Chapter Six

Games

USED TO FIGHT a great deal with the Indian boys and I could whip any of them that were my age. When I would whip one of them, his mother and the rest of the women would tease him because he had let me get the best of him.

We used to wrestle by the hour. The Indians themselves, even the grown men, used to wrestle a good deal.

The Indians used to joke among themselves, and some of the jokes, especially among the young men, were pretty rough. I remember that when the women were gathering gooseberries and blackberries, they would try to get me to eat many of the other kinds of berries that grew along the river. Some of these were awfully bitter, and some little short of poison, and they would laugh and laugh when I would try to eat some of them.

I used to play many games with the Indian boys and with the grown Indians. The boys used to make dummy ducks, or fish, of bark and throw them in the river. As they floated downstream, we

would shoot arrows at them or practice throwing a
spear at them. Where the water was
shallow we would wade in and re-
cover our weapons. Sometimes we
would follow the floating dummy
a great distance down the river.

The Indian boys used a sling
exactly like the white boys use, but I never saw a grown Indian use
one. It was made of buckskin, a piece of skin about three inches
square with two strings about two and one-half feet long fastened to
it. One string had a loop on the loose end. They placed the loop over
one finger and held the end of the other string in the same hand.
They gave the sling one fast whirl and let go of the string. The boys
liked to see who could throw rocks up the river farthest. I never saw
them try to kill anything with a sling.

Each rancheria had a gaming court at, or near, its center. This
court was made by smoothing the earth and tamping it solid. It was
then covered with fine sand, and many games were played upon it.
Here was always an excited, shouting, yelling, laughing group, generally including men, women and children, all intent upon their game
and as carefree and happy as it is possible for human beings to be.

The game I remember best was played with a hoop and a pole
about ten feet long. The hoop was made of bark coiled into a flat disc,
held together with slender willow shoots, and covered with untanned
buckskin. The hoop was about one and one-half feet in diameter and
had a hole in the center about two or three inches in diameter.

Buckskin sling

Any and everyone played this game. Sides were chosen and one person from each team was selected to roll the hoop. These two persons stood about twenty or thirty yards apart and at each end of the game court. They rolled the hoop back and forth between them. The game was to throw a pole through the hoop as it rolled by. For each pole thrown through the hoop, two points were awarded. If the pole only knocked the hoop over, it counted as one point. The players lined up on each side of the course where the hoop was rolled. They laughed and yelled and made a great deal of noise at this game and did all they could to rattle the opposing players when they were about to throw a pole.

This was a great deal more exciting game that you might think just from reading about it. When the hoop was rolled across the court as many as thirty or forty poles would go flying through the air and the biggest problem in the game was to dodge the poles that came from the other side. They kept the score by calling it aloud much as we keep score in a game of horseshoes.

The women had a dice game that was played on a large mat or flat basket. The dice were made of nut shells or acorn caps filled with pitch and decorated on the flat side with small pieces of shell. I have seen them play this game by the hour, but I really knew very little about it. The dice were gathered up in the hand and rolled out on the basket. If two or seven flat sides remained up when the dice had stopped rolling, a point was scored.

The men had a sort of guessing game which they called *ha-nów-ish*. They sat facing each other. One person held two small sticks in his hand, one of which was marked. He would put his hands behind him and shuffle the sticks back and forth from one hand to the other. Finally he would bring his hands to the front, and the person opposite attempted to guess in which hand he held the marked stick. They kept score with small sticks called *wé-chet*. If the one guessing failed to guess the proper hand, he lost to the person holding the stick. If he guessed right, he won a point.

One of the most amusing games played by the Indians was a sort of football game called *tah-lúh-wush*. A round stone about two or two and one-half inches in diameter was used. This stone was often very round and nicely polished. The stone was not kicked: the toes were caught under it and it was thrown forward. Sides were chosen and goals arranged. Sometimes two trees about two hundred yards apart would be used for goals, or sticks might be planted for goals.

Everyone played, and they surely made a rough-house of it. One person started the ball. A point was scored when the stone was brought in contact with the goal of the opponents. They used to push, shove, hold, trip, and wrestle. Sometimes, when the ball was near a goal, both sides would crowd close like a band of milling sheep. Then the ball might come rolling out between the many feet and someone would pass it to the other goal before the mass could break up and stop the play.

A small, round gourd used to grow on the San Joaquin Valley plains. I have seen hundreds of acres of sandy soil along the rivers covered with the gourd plant. It put out long, tapering, pointed stems with yellow flowers and green gourds, as round as baseballs and slightly larger. Except during the hottest part of the day you would probably see from a half-dozen to forty Indian children playing football with these gourds. Sometimes there would be several games going at one time.

The Indians also played a game exactly like the game of shinny [hockey] played by white boys today. It was generally played by young men from fourteen to twenty years of age. A wooden ball was used and a club was prepared. This club was curved on one end. This game was scored in the same way as the football game. It was a rough game, and the Indians sometimes were badly bruised in playing it.

Chapter Seven

The Way We Lived:
Indian Customs and Public Life

THESE INDIANS generally married at about the age of twenty years, never at a younger age than fifteen or sixteen. The young man would talk with the parents of the intended bride. Then he would talk to the girl. I rather believe, from one or two things that I saw, that there was often an understanding beforehand between the young man and the intended bride, but I cannot be sure. After the parents of the bride had talked the matter over and had decided that the young man was all right, they notified him. Then he went away for a short distance, sometimes only a few yards, sometimes a half-mile or more, and built a house for his bride.

When the house was finished they started housekeeping. I know of no ceremony, but they said they were married. I am sure that in the tribe that I lived with it was not customary for the new couple to live with either of the parents-in-law. Neither do I know of any rules against the son-in-law talking to his mother-in-law, as I understand was customary among many of the valley tribes.

The Indians that I knew lived at old Millerton on the San Joaquin River, above Centerville on Kings River, down Kings River to Tulare Lake, and on the north shore of that lake. A person might find that the things I learned from them would not apply to all other tribes in the valley.

Houses

There was considerable difference between the houses built by different tribes. On Tulare Lake a long house was built of a thin layer of tules, but on Kings River quite a permanent building was constructed. They would dig a hole in the ground to a depth of as much as two feet. This hole would be about circular, from ten to twenty feet in diameter. The soil was loosened with pointed sticks and carried out in baskets. The soil removed was thrown out around the sides of the hole. Then long, slender willow poles would be planted in the bottom of this hole, next to the walls.

Willow frame for tule house

Frame covered with tule reeds

These poles would be placed about six inches apart.

A space about two feet wide was left for a door at the south side of the house. A willow hoop about two and one-half feet in diameter was made. The poles were bent together at the tops and tied to the hoop. Then more long, slender poles were bent around the outside of the upright poles and tied to them about two feet apart. This made a beehive-shaped wickerwork frame. Around and over this frame were stood tules to a depth of about ten or twelve inches. Then the soil was thrown over the tules to a depth of several inches.

After a few years the grass grew over the house and it looked like an underground house or cellar. In bad weather the fire was kindled in the middle of the house, under the round hole which had been left at the top. Some of the smoke found its way out through the hole above. There was no other opening except the door.

Tule house covered with grass

The house was used only in bad weather except for sleeping. Otherwise cooking and eating and all preparation of materials would be carried on outside. The floor of the house would be covered with several thicknesses of tule mats. Around the inside of the wall tule mats would be piled up to a thickness of several inches. These served as a mattress for sleeping. When they could be obtained, grizzly bear skins were used on top of the mattress. In very cold weather a rabbitskin blanket would be used in addition to the bearskin. Then, too, in cold weather some of the old people would be up most of the night rebuilding the fire. When I awakened I would see them moving quietly about and sometimes talking to each other in low tones.

Near the house there was generally a shallow pit in which a fire was kept burning most of the time. In the evenings or during cold weather they would sit about it rather than go in the house. They were outside almost all of the time. All of the camp refuse was thrown in the fire pit. When an Indian washed his face and hands he would go to the fire and stand there until he was dry. They used no towels, and none were necessary when the skin was dried by the fire immediately.

The Indians did not eat at regular hours, except possibly the evening meal. They had no lamps and they made it a practice to have all their work and their last eating done about sundown. The hunters would come in shortly before that time and generally everyone would gather around for a meal.

In the morning, after the dip in the river, the population of an Indian rancheria generally scattered. The men would visit all of their traps and snares to see what had been caught during the night. Even

the small boys would have snares set. Some of the men would go hunting, some fishing, and some to work on things that they might be making. Some of the women would go into the hills after roots and other materials for weaving or basketry, or along the river to gather berries, or on the plains and hills to harvest seeds. Gradually everyone would wander back to the rancheria late in the morning. They would eat in turn as they wandered in.

Babies

Babies and small children were carried on the backs of the women, in a sort of wicker basket cradle. The basket cradle was a handy means of caring for the baby. When the babies were strapped to the baskets, the women always knew where to look for them. They kept some of the children strapped to the baskets a part of the time until they were at least two years old.

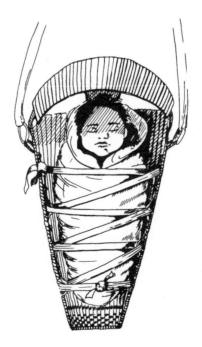

The Choinumne used three kinds of cradles for their children. The first was a light, flexible mat that could be rolled up. A large cradle was used when the child was about six or eight weeks old. It was made by bending a long withe [stick] into a "u" shape about a foot across and two feet long. It had a woven sunshade over it, and was carried on the woman's back by means of a flat strap made of wild milkweed fiber which crossed her forehead. Sometimes she placed an ornamented basket cap under the strap.

Another cradle was made of a forked stick with crossed sticks tied to it. It was also carried by a fiber strap. The ends of these willow cross-sticks projected a couple of inches beyond each side. Then the framework was covered with woven grass or other materials, and the child was lashed to it, the hands being lashed down at the sides. The lashing was done with a milkweed string which was looped over the projecting ends of the cross-sticks and was crossed over the child, much the same as a shoe is laced.

Padding of bark and moss or soft grass was placed under the child, and a light skin, or a rabbitskin blanket in cold weather, was wrapped around it. The child was taken to the stream near camp several times a day, removed from the basket, and washed.

When the child was being carried, which was most of the time, it was suspended by a sort of woven belt made of milkweed string. This belt was passed under the basket and around the forehead of the woman. When the load was heavy, the woman wore a small basket over her head like a skull cap, the same as she would when carrying acorns.

Chiefs

I remember that the chief, or headman, of the tribe used to give orders about the gathering of the supply of food. He was held more or less responsible for the well-being of the whole tribe, and I believe he would have been in disgrace had he allowed the tribe to become in want. He had to settle all of the quarrels and differences between different members of the tribe, and still be fair and friendly to everyone concerned.

On the whole, the Indians I was with quarreled very little. An Indian can say less with more grace than anyone you will meet. The adult Indians very seldom ever quarreled or even argued with each other. In general they did very little useless talking. They were not as quiet as many people suppose, but were not inclined to talk or gossip carelessly. I remember only one or two quarrels between men, and only one between women. The Indians I lived with always joked among themselves, and they all enjoyed themselves. The women were treated well by their husbands.

I am not sure how the Choinumne selected their chiefs. I was not with them long enough to watch them choose a new chief. But I am sure that if a chief did not perform his duties well, the Indians would have selected someone else to take his place. They would not actually vote him out, but they would simply turn to someone they considered wiser. I may be wrong about this, but I am judging from what I saw of the Choinumne's lives. In general, chiefs were selected because they were seen as the wisest members of the tribe, and people naturally went to them for advice.

The oldest son of the chief held a rather important position, at least in the tribe I was with. He was generally included in any important talks, and was consulted when anything of importance was to be decided. From what I heard of their consultations I would judge that the oldest son was being prepared to be a headman, and would eventually have taken his father's place.

The year before I left the Indians I was about sixteen, and I remember that there was some discussion as to whether I was to be initiated into the tribe at the time when several other boys were initiated. However, it was not done, and my daddy took me from them before the time came around again the next year. In a way I have always regretted this, as I saw practically nothing of the initiation of the other boys the year before, and have always wished that I knew just what they said and did at the initiation. At the time of the initiation ceremonies, I do remember that the young boys were coached by one or two of the older men who used to tell us stories during the evenings around the fire. But I saw nothing of any sort of a ceremony.

Bathing

White people generally have a wrong impression as to how the Indians bathed together in the rivers. In the first place, before sunup practically every Indian at the rancheria had taken a bath: men, women and children.

At the morning bath the men generally removed the breechcloth and bathed before the women were up. During the day, at least in summer, when they would be in the water from one to twenty times, the breechcloth was left in place and was worn while it was drying.

Children were taught not to fear the water. I have seen the women take their babies down to the river when they were only a few days old. They would hold them on their open hands and dip their backs in the water. If the child was startled by the water they would talk to it and reassure it. Then they would dip it in again and again until it was not afraid to go completely under.

Sometimes when the baby was dipped under the water it would come up coughing, but the mother would talk to it and dip it in again until it lost all fear. They would then teach it to swim by holding it partly out of the water.

Many of the Indian children could swim almost as soon as they could walk. In fact, many of the children were kept strapped on the cradle so long that I believe they could swim before they could walk.

The women considered it a disgrace that I could not swim when I first went to live with them, and they soon made me learn how. They did not help me, but made me go out in the shallow water and imitate the other children until I learned how. I soon learned how to swim as well as any of them. We thought nothing of plunging into the river anyplace we wanted to cross. I never saw or heard of an accidental drowning among the Indians.

Sometimes the women would place a child in the deep water alone long before it could walk. They would bend a willow branch down to the water and allow the child to hold on to it. Then they would go on about their work, and sometimes pay no attention to it for a quarter of an hour or more. I remember that once I thought I would have some fun, and when the woman was some distance away

I shook the limb the child was clinging to. It never made a noise, but gave the blackest look I ever received.

Sickness and Death

The Indian doctors treated their patients by bloodletting. They would make a cut and suck out some blood. They also had another peculiar treatment. They would twist together some wormwood leaves and set them afire. With the glowing end of this firebrand, a stripe was burned along each side of the spinal column of the patient. They also did a great deal of howling over the patient. When a doctor had lost several patients, the relatives of the last deceased had the right to kill him. He was shot with arrows, or stoned to death, and made no resistance. An Indian doctor was considered *trip-nee*, which means supernatural.

In general, the young people and children were very respectful to old people. I do not remember having seen an old person slighted, or treated disrespectfully by anyone. Of course, when old people became helpless they would do nothing for them, and sometimes they suffered a great deal. I have heard white people tell about the Indians abandoning old people in order to allow them to die, and also about them being buried alive, but I never saw anything like that done.

The bodies were prepared for burial by being tied with the knees under the chin and the arms doubled at the sides. The grave was dug with the pointed sticks used in digging grass nuts. The soil was carried out in baskets. Everyone, except the close relations, helped to dig the grave.

The mourning generally went on for several days. They would stand around the grave as it was being filled and cry and moan. Sometimes they would keep this up day and night. The mother or wife of the dead person cut her hair and put on pitch and charcoal.

Chapter Eight

What We Ate: Indian Cooking

T HE INDIANS ALWAYS had a supply of food stored up. An Indian might go out and hunt all morning, or all day, and not get any game, but he could always come home and get something to eat.

Lots of wild oat seed was prepared and eaten each year. This was an important food to the Choinumnes. The seed was gathered with a basket and a fan-shaped wicker seed-beater. The woman held the basket in the hollow of her left arm and the seed-beater in her right hand. She walked about among the oats, holding the basket below the heads with the its mouth sloping forward. With the seed-beater she thrashed the seed into the basket. Many other seeds were gathered in the same way.

The oats were stored in baskets and skin bags and prepared as they were needed. They were generally parched on a flat tray. Hot rocks or coals were put on the tray with the oats. The tray was shaken until the covering was burned from the seed, and the seed

*Gathering
wild oat seeds*

itself was browned. The seed was then winnowed and looked a lot like wheat that was badly shrunken.

Sometimes they parched the oats and other seeds in stone mortars. I have seen them parch seed in iron kettles they obtained from the whites. The parched seed was pounded in a mortar and was cooked in a basket with water and hot rocks to form a gruel or mush much like acorn mush.

Inside the house would be stored acorns, dried fish, dried game, dried grasses, and many kinds of seeds. Outside was an acorn granary [storage building]. The granary was built to hold many bushels of acorns and was used only at permanent villages. Four poles about ten or fifteen feet long were planted in the ground in the form of a square about four feet across. Around these were woven willow shoots. A bottom was woven into the sides about two feet from the ground. The inside of this wicker frame was lined with tules or a grass which the squirrels did not like. The acorns were poured in at the open top from the baskets in which they had been carried from the hills. When some acorns were wanted from the granary the grass would be pulled apart near the bottom and the acorns would run out into a basket. They would then be carried to a shady place to be hulled.

It was really a lot of work to prepare acorns for use. The women did all of this. First they gathered the acorns in the woods and filled their tall, cone-shaped baskets with them. They fitted a net made of milkweed string around this basket. To this net was fastened a long strap woven of milkweed string. The basket full of acorns was placed on the back and the strap passed around in front of the forehead. In this way the acorns were carried as far as two or three miles to the granary.

The acorns were hulled on a large, flat rock in the shade by the stream. They were stood on end on the rock and the top was struck with another rock. The dry hull would crack open and fall away. In the large, flat rock were many holes where the hulled acorns were ground into flour. A few hulled acorns were thrown into one of these holes, or mortars, and pounded with a long, slender rock, or pestle. The flour was brushed from the mortar with a brush made of soaproot husk, and placed in a sort of sieve, or colander, made of fine willow shoots. In this it was sifted and the coarse particles were returned to the mortar.

A large flat rock with holes (mortars) was used for hulling and pounding acorns.

Next a hollow basin about a foot or more across was made in the sand by the stream. The acorn flour was mixed with water and pounded into this basin. Then several basketfuls of hot water were poured over it. The hot water carried [leached] the bitterness from the flour down into the sand below. The wet flour was then allowed to stand until it had dried into a large cake. When dry it was lifted from its bed and the sand brushed from it. In this condition it was used as bread.

From the acorn bread was also made a sort of soup. The bread was broken up and mixed with a large quantity of water. This was all heated.

All boiling was done in baskets. These baskets were made by the women and were watertight. They had very pretty designs woven into them. Rocks were heated in the fire and dropped into a basket of water or soup. A looped stick was used to handle the rocks and to stir the contents of the basket. This stick was made of an oak limb, doubled in the middle and its two ends fastened together. A small loop was left at the other end. The hot rocks would be caught between two green sticks and lifted into the basket. Then the contents of the basket would be stirred with the looped end of the stick. When the heat had passed from the rock, it was again caught in the loop and put back in the fire.

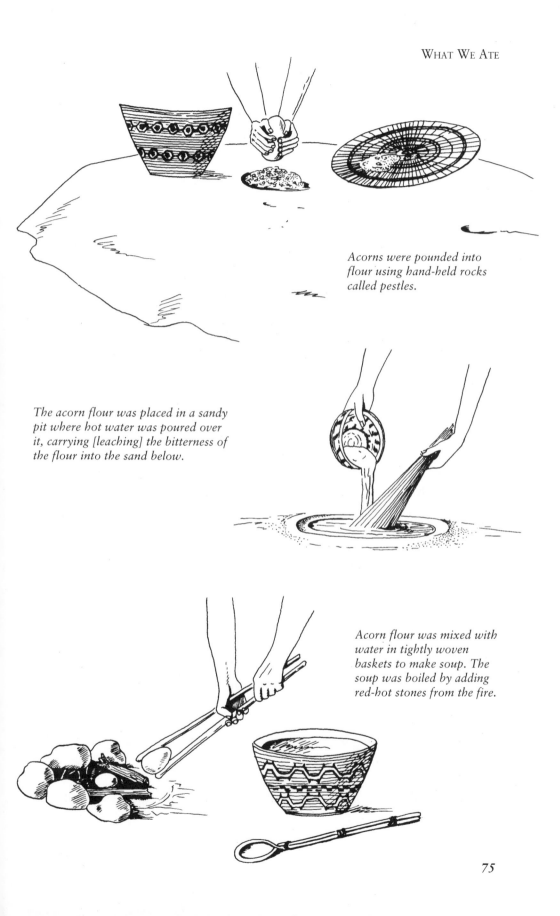

Acorns were pounded into flour using hand-held rocks called pestles.

The acorn flour was placed in a sandy pit where hot water was poured over it, carrying [leaching] the bitterness of the flour into the sand below.

Acorn flour was mixed with water in tightly woven baskets to make soup. The soup was boiled by adding red-hot stones from the fire.

The only cooking or kitchen utensils I ever saw the Indians use were baskets and mortars. They used small baskets for dippers, and around camp they drank from them.

They had many kinds of baskets. They made a sort of colander of cottonwood twigs, a tray, large cooking baskets, a large, cone-shaped carrying basket, a small basket used as a drinking cup, and so on. Most of these baskets had very pretty designs on them, almost every kind of design you could think of. When they were soaked in water they would not leak, and they were almost as strong as sheet iron.

The Indians kept most of their belongings in baskets and in bags. Their bags were made by gathering up the edges of an irregularly shaped piece of elk or buckskin and tying a string around it. They were of many sizes, from a size that would hold a hundred pounds of acorns down to a size they could hold in the palm of the hand.

When there was an acorn shortage, the seed of the buckeye was prepared and eaten. These were poisonous and the meal made from the seed had to be leached much longer than the acorn flour. The leaves of the manzanita were also powdered and mixed with the buckeye flour, and this helped to reduce the bitterness. Otherwise the buckeye bread was prepared the same as the acorn bread. The manzanita berry was also eaten.

A sweet cider was made from the juice of the manzanita berries. They were crushed in mortars and set in wicker colanders to drain into baskets. A little water was added to the crushed berries. This made a sweet and well-flavored cider, and I remember it with more relish than anything I ever ate or drank with the Indians.

They ate great quantities of young tule roots, which were soft and sweet. The lake Indians made an almost pure starch from tule roots. The women waded into the water and dug the roots out with pointed sticks. Other women pulled the roots out onto the bank. There the women cut the roots from the stalks.

The roots were thrown into stone mortars and were pounded into a soft mass. The pounded roots were then thrown into a large cooking basket and were covered with hot water. The mixture was stirred with the looped stirring stick for an hour or so. Then the crushed roots were raked out and were thrown away. In an hour or two, the starch had settled to the bottom of the basket. The water was then poured off. They obtained in this way a cake of starch two inches in thickness, and eight or nine inches in diameter. It had very little taste but was very rich. They also ate the tule roots.

At Tulare Lake, great quantities of grass nuts were gathered and eaten. These grew underground in the sandy places, particularly about the lake. They had a bunch of stickers on the top and a sort of husk or hull on them, and grew on a long root, like beads on a string. The hull was black and the nut sweet and rich. The Indians also ate the bulbs of certain wildflowers, and when the stems of the flowers had dried the women would go out over the hillsides and dig them by the bushel.

The Indians would not eat a coyote. I never knew why, but I am sure there was some reason for it.

Pine nuts were eaten in great quantities. After two or three hundred pounds of pine cones had been gathered, they were piled up and

fired. The cones were covered with pitch, and this made them burn easily. It was almost impossible to remove the nuts in any other way. The cones were covered with sharp spines and were so solid that they could not be opened with anything the Indians had. The coating of pitch also made them hard to handle. I have always figured that the pitch was a part of the effort of nature to keep squirrels and other pests away from the nuts. After the outside of the cones had been burned a little, they began to curl open and the nuts would become loose. The Indians would use a stick to rake the cones out of the fire and knock the nuts out. Finally they would have a pile of about fifteen or twenty pounds of nuts for their trouble. These they cracked and ate as they were, partly roasted. Some of the nuts they would mash and make into mush. This mush was very rich, and a person could eat only a small amount of it.

Everyone—men, women and children—might eat at the same time and together. They all ate from the same basket, dipping the food out with the three first fingers of the right hand, but they generally ate when they felt hungry and generally ate alone.

Indians were very careful about polluting a stream near their rancheria or camp. If they had to wade the stream they would do so below the camp, or they might cross on rocks above. The sweat house was located below camp and all bathing was done there. They would very seldom wash their hands and face in a stream. When drinking from a stream they would arise with their mouths full of water. They would allow this water to run over their hands and would in that way wash their hands and faces away from the stream. One mouthful of water would wash hands and face and leave some to spare.

When rock salt could be obtained, it was used for seasoning. The Choinumne sometimes used a salt stick instead. The bark was peeled from a small willow limb. This limb was whipped about in the salt grass that grew in great quantities. On the leaves of the salt grass were many small particles of sticky salt. A coating of this salt was accumulated on the stick. The Indians would pull a handful of sweet clover, roll it into a ball between the palms of their hands, and stuff it into their mouths. Then after it had been chewed, the salt stick was drawn through the mouth. They also ate mustard, miner's lettuce, and many other greens, both raw and cooked. The salt from the salt grass was dried and was also used for seasoning. It had a sour, salty taste, a good deal like a dill pickle.

Rock salt was highly valued by the Choinumne and had to be obtained in trade from the Paiutes, who got it by boiling down the waters of Owens Lake. They filled a basket with lake water, heated rocks and held them in the water until cool. This they continued until a cake of mineral salt about the size of a soup plate was obtained.

Small game was roasted in the ashes and coals, leaving the skin on. When the meat was done the skin would be stripped off and the squirrel or quail would be as clean and nice as you would want it. Many times the entrails were eaten. They were split open and washed and stewed or broiled over the coals.

Meat was broiled on the end of a long, slender withe. The big end of the withe would be set in the ground at some distance from the fire, and the meat hung on the other end. The weight of the meat bent the withe over until the meat hung directly over the fire, or coals. In this way the heat from the fire would not burn the withe.

After the evening meal they would all lie around the fire on the ground through the long evening and tell stories and sing until as late as ten or eleven o'clock. This was the finest part of their lives. Here was the real family circle. The long evenings were spent about the fires in the most pleasant way imaginable. Every night was a bonfire party. The old sages would tell stories about their own experiences when they were young, or about the history of their tribe, or just simple stories they may have made up. We youngsters would sit around with our mouths and eyes and ears open and listen until we had to go to bed.

Three musical instruments were used, sometimes all at once, and sometimes as an accompaniment to singing. They used a sort of flute made of a hollow elder limb. This made a shrill, whistling sound. I never heard the Indians themselves whistle except in signaling to one another.

They had a clapper made of a split stick. They struck this against something in time to the flute. Or, instead of the clapper, they sometimes beat on a section of log with any stick that came handy. I believe that some of these logs were hollow, or had been hollowed out on the underside.

Probably the best-sounding musical instrument was a short bow. It was smaller than their hunting bow. They placed one end of the back of this against their teeth and thumbed the string like one would a guitar, raising and lowering the pitch with the mouth. This music used to accompany their singing. Some of their songs were quite monotonous, but some of them were very pretty.

When the men were hunting they sometimes used to go along with their bows strung and play them in the same way as they did the musical instrument, using an arrow to strike the string.

As the evening wore on, and various individuals grew tired or sleepy, they would wander off to bed. We would go inside and lie down on the tule mattresses next to the walls of the house with our feet to the fire and cover up with a rabbitskin blanket, or whatever the weather demanded. We slept in the clothing we had been wearing during the day. We had no shoes or other clothing to take off unless the weather was extremely cold, when we might have a wildcat or mountain-lion skin about our shoulders.

Chapter Nine

What We Wore: Indian Clothing

MANY PEOPLE do not know how the breechcloth and gee string were made and used. A strip about ten inches wide was cut out of the middle of a deer skin, using the longest portion, from the neck to the tail. This strip was called by the white people a "breech clout," or breechcloth. The gee string was a narrow string of buckskin long enough to pass around the waist and tie.

The breechcloth was folded across the middle of the gee string much as a towel would be folded across a clothesline. It was then placed behind the wearer, and the ends of the gee string brought around to the front. The ends of the breechcloth were brought between the legs to the front and held against the heart, under the chin. The ends of the gee string were tied over the front of the breechcloth. Then the ends of the breechcloth were allowed to drop down and hang loose in front, like a small apron.

This completed the wearing apparel of the men except in cold weather, when a mountain-lion skin might be tied about the shoulders. They wore no foot covering of any sort and had no word in their language for anything of the kind. Their feet were as tough as any shoe.

Young children wore no clothing at all, but I have seen many white families who thought nothing of letting their children run around without clothing.

The women wore a rabbitskin skirt woven together like the blanket. This was made of two aprons, one in front and one behind. The apron behind was smaller than that in front. These aprons reached about to the knees of the wearers.

Both men and women wore their hair long. I do not believe that it was customary for them to braid their hair in the days before they came in contact with the white people. I never saw one of the real old Indians with braided hair. Neither did the Indians naturally shake hands. They hugged each other about the shoulders like Frenchmen, an act they called *cáw-bush*.

The women cut their hair off in front in bangs, but the men left their hair long across the front. Both men and women sometimes smeared their hair with bear oil, which made it shine.

The Indians had little or no beard. The young men pulled it out with a sort of tweezers made of a split stick until it did not grow in again to any great extent. Some of the men allowed their moustaches to grow.

To brush the hair, the Indians used a very good brush made of the husk of the tall soaproot. It had curved bristles. Another such brush was made with straight bristles and was used for brushing the acorn flour out of the mortars. One end of the husk was tied with milkweed string to make the brush. Then the mashed pulp of the bulb about which the husk had grown was placed over the handle. This dried and kept the fiber of the husk from loosening and falling out. This same pulp was used to waterproof and sunproof the cover for the baby cradle by means of which the babies were carried on the backs of the women.

A common article about an Indian house was a dried goose or duck wing. It was dried partly spread open and was used as a brush. It made a very good one, too. I remember that the Indians gave Mother one. She used it to brush crumbs off the table.

The paint used by the Indians I knew was red and white. They would paint their faces red and then paint white stripes across them. As a sign of mourning, the women used to cover their faces and hair with a mixture of pine pitch and charcoal. Some of the near relatives also cut their hair short as a sign of mourning.

The women used to tattoo their chins. They would make cuts on their chins with small, sharp chips of rock and rub charcoal into the cuts. I do not know of any reason for the painting or tattooing, except that I believe the men used to paint up for special occasions.

Both men and women wore beads around their necks. Some of the women pierced their noses. After piercing, a woman would run a slim piece of shell or bone through her nose. This piece of bone would be five or six inches long. Most of them pierced their ears and wore shells in them.

Chapter Ten

Morals

THERE IS NO USE trying to deny that the Indians I knew were, for the most part, called "savages" by those who didn't know them yet. But there was nothing in the Indian language that compared with our profanity and vulgarity. They did not have the indecent attitude that white people have. They had no cash registers or padlocks. Everything they possessed was left in the open and was safe from being stolen or being molested in any way.

The Indians, even the children, were very modest in their ideas about their own abilities. But I remember exceptions. A boy about fifteen years of age was called *Búh-sho*, which meant "braggart." Another was named *Múh-loosh*, which meant "cheat." Another Indian boy was very nosy. He was always watching anything that was going on. His name was *Bo-có-lah*, meaning "snooper."

I seldom ever knew the Indians to cheat at anything. I remember that when we played their game of water tag, some of the Indian boys would swim deep into the muddy water and I would have to go

down after them. As soon as I touched one of them, he would immediately come up and take my place. I did not know whom I had tagged, but there was never any argument. And when I was down I never had one claim he had touched me when he had not. I never remember hearing an argument of any kind in an Indian game. I remember that when I started school near Venice Hill with the white boys in 1862, I was surprised to find I could not trust them to tell the truth when we played water tag. So I quit playing it with them.

The Indians had their own ideas of proper manners. It was very bad manners to be impolite to old people. In fact, children were almost never impolite to old people. When an Indian woman had something choice to give to the children, probably sugar-pine sugar or candy she had traded for at Centerville, she would say, *"Joul-bú-sho,"* which meant "I have something to divide up." All the children within hearing would come on the run. But they would not crowd each other. They would wait their turn. And each got an equal share. If one put himself before the others, the Indian woman would say, *"Ta-míd-um,"* meaning "Where are your manners?" The child would be so embarrassed he would refuse his portion and would go and hide. If a child upset a basket of acorn mush or got into something he shouldn't, which was very seldom, his mother would say, *"To-trá-shee-uh."* *To-tree* meant bad; so she said, "That is bad business."

The average Indian I knew was more reliable than the average white man I knew in after years. They knew how to make fermented liquor, because their sweet manzanita wine would ferment when they kept it too long. But it was thrown out when it fermented. I never knew an Indian to make any sort of fermented liquor to drink. The first person who ever offered me a drink of fermented liquor was a white man.

The Indians knew the use of tobacco, but they used it sparingly. I do not believe that an Indian naturally smoked more than one or two puffs in three or four days.

They also knew the use of a strong drug, the tea from the root of the Jimson weed. But it was used only once in a lifetime, when a young man was being initiated into the tribe. I never saw or heard of an Indian using a native drug habitually.

The moral conditions in the Indian rancheria where I stayed were better than they were in the white villages that grew up nearby. They were better there in the 1860s than they were in any of the rest of the towns I knew in those days, or since. I do not mean that everyone in the white towns was bad, but that a great many things went on there that were unheard of at the rancheria.

The reason that my daddy left me with the Indians until I was about seventeen, instead of taking me from them when I was old enough to take care of myself, was because he said that I was in better company with the Indians than I would be staying around the white towns with him. There I would be in contact with saloons, gamblers, drunks, bums, and many other undesirables that I would not know at the rancheria.

Many of the white settlers of the 1860s might disagree with me about the things I am mentioning. But they could not, and never did, know those Indians in their natural state.

Chapter Eleven

Fishing and Hunting

THE INDIANS on the San Joaquin and Kings Rivers used to catch fish with a pointed net made of milkweed string and fastened to a willow hoop. This they set in the river with the mouth upstream. To it they added wings of willow wicker construction. Then they drove the fish downstream into the net.

The Indians trapped lots of fish. They built the trap of small, green limbs. It had wings extending to each side of the river and was located just below a riffle [a small rapid]. Between the wings was a hole. In the deep water below and connected to the hole was a long, basket-like trap. It was about three feet in diameter and eighteen or twenty feet long.

The Indians would go upstream from the trap and build a sort of drag to scare the fish down into the trap. They tied oak limbs end to end until they reached across the river. Then they tied the butts of brush to the oak limbs. The fish could not get through the brush.

When the drag was completed, the Indians would pull on each end of the oak limbs and draw the affair downstream. The current would help force it down to the trap. The brush would comb the fish out of the holes. When they arrived at the riffle, the fish could be seen flopping over into the trap. The trap would be filled almost solid with fish. They would catch hundreds in one drive.

Some of the fish they would eat fresh, and some they would dry. Not a fish went to waste. They would fasten the trap to the bank and keep some of the fish in it and eat them fresh for a long time.

They also caught fish in pools with a wicker basket. This basket was three feet or more in diameter at the large end, about eighteen inches high, and eight inches across the small end, which was left open. They would wade quietly in a pool until they could see a fish. Then they would clap the basket, large end down, over it. The fish thus trapped would be removed by reaching through the small open end of the basket. They would bite the top of the head off the fish and throw it out on the bank.

Trout and other large fish were speared with a gig. It had a long, slender pole for a handle. This pole was made of elderberry wood, often twenty feet long and about an inch in diameter. It would be as straight as an arrow, and as smooth as glass. Fishermen took a great deal of pride in the fish gigs and would keep them polished until they were shiny.

Ground squirrels were quite plentiful and, as I have mentioned before, in some places the ground was cast up into great mounds by them. The Indians used to kill these squirrels by smoking them out. A party of a dozen or more of the men would go out on the plains for a squirrel hunt. They would select one of the large dens where there were hundreds of squirrels. They would fill the tops of all the holes in a large den with earth, except four or five of the main ones. Then they would stuff grass and weeds in the open holes and set fire to them. A basket or skin would be used to fan and force the smoke into the holes.

After the holes had been filled with smoke the ones through which the smoke had been forced would be filled with earth. Then the people who had been doing the smoking would sit down in the shade for a couple of hours and sleep, or play their guessing game. If they were near the river, sometimes they would fish.

When the holes were opened, the squirrels would be found dead near the top, where they had tried to get out to the fresh air. The hunters would tuck the heads of the squirrels under their gee strings, which were tied tightly around their waists. Sometimes all of the hunters would have a complete girdle of squirrels. I remember seeing them come in that way many times when I was very young, and later I hunted squirrels with them. Ground squirrels were almost the best and the most unfailing of their food sources.

They trapped quail in a wicker basket by means of a low fence. The basket was placed at an opening in the fence. The quail would run along the fence rather than fly over it and would enter the basket through the opening.

There was quite a variety of food for the Indians to eat. In addition to the things I have already mentioned were mud hens, ducks, geese, larks, sandhill cranes, swans, rabbits, raccoons, antelope, elk, deer, gophers, many kinds of roots and seeds, and other things of minor importance.

The Indian families were fairly small, three to four children, rarely as many as five. So it was easy for the head of the family to provide game, and for the woman to gather plenty of seeds and acorns.

Hunting squirrels

Chapter Twelve

Native Wildlife

THERE WERE ABOUT six kinds of geese in the San Joaquin when I first came here, and there were probably billions of them. I have seen the white geese with black wing tips flying so thickly that I am positive one band of them would cover four square miles of land as thick as they could land and take off again. The Indians trapped these geese at Tulare Lake, but I never saw it done. I liked to hunt antelope, elk, raccoons, and deer better than to hunt any kind of waterfowl or to fish, but I have seen forty Indians come in from the swamps at one time, loaded down with all the white geese they could carry. I have also seen the nets the Indians used to catch geese and ducks, but I know nothing about them, except that they were made of string, were tied something like a fish net, and were fastened to light willow poles.

There were mallard ducks, teal ducks, and wood ducks, (all known as *wáts-wats*) which nested in hollow trees and were the most beautiful bird in the country. And there were blackbirds, blue jays, crested

Wáts-wats
(Wood duck)

jays, condors, buzzards, blue birds, blue fish cranes, sandhill cranes, and bald eagles which were sacred to the Choinumne. There were also black eagles, crows, and red-tailed hawks. They had a name for every bug or bird or animal that walked or crawled or hopped or flew, and every grown Indian knew every one of them.

There used to be a sort of fish in Tulare Lake that must have been an eel. Other fish included trout, steelhead trout, suckers, and salmon.

The Indians often had pet deer around camp. They would capture fawns and feed them on acorn soup and keep them around camp until they were grown or until the first mating season, and then they would seldom be seen again.

The Indians had always had pet dogs. When I was with the Indians on the upper Kings River, they still had some dogs that they claimed had not been mixed with white people's dogs. These were about as big as, but heavier than, an average coyote, and were about the same color. Their hair was shorter and thicker. Their ears were not so erect, and their noses not so pointed. They could easily have been mistaken for coyotes.

Sím-sim
(Bat)

Many of the white people thought that there were five kinds of bears in the mountains. They thought there were two kinds of grizzlies, one a silvertip, which was nothing more than the common grizzly with his full winter coat. Then they thought there were brown, black and cinnamon bears. The Indians observed everything about them too closely ever to be deceived about such things. They knew that the last three bears came from the same mother. They had just two words: *náw-hawn* for grizzly and *mo-hó-o* for black bear.

I knew the Choinumne names for all of the animals, but I suppose I have forgotten all but the common ones. "Antelope" was *súey-all*, "porcupine" was *pów-putch*, and "badger" was *trúh-now*. The Indians were always interested in bats and had many stories about them, but I did not learn them. The children who ran with me around the rancheria used to hunt for bat roosts and capture the bats. The name for bat was *sím-sim*, and was an imitation of the squeak made by them. There were also beavers, golden mantle squirrels, chipmunks, cottontails, jackrabbits, elk, fox, mink, raccoons, wildcats, gray squirrels, and wolves.

The Indians always imagined that bad, mean animals were in the woods, imagi-

Trúh-now
(Badger)

99

nary ones that no one ever saw. Young people liked to scare each other, especially at night. They used the word *peesh* to indicate these imaginary beasts. After I had been gone from the Indians for ten years, I would still jump out of my skin if anyone yelled *"peesh!"* behind me in the dark woods.

Chapter Thirteen

Hunting Lore

HE INDIAN did not hold his bow like a white man does. It was short and was held diagonally. The arrow was placed on top of the bow, which would be opposite to the method used by modern archers. I believe that this was because they stalked much of their game and a long bow, or one held perpendicularly, would be seen too easily.

An Indian could shoot from cover without exposing more than the point of the arrow and one eye. He turned his head to one side and sighted along the top of the arrow.

An Indian hunter was always cranky about anyone handling his bows or arrows. He kept his bow in a case made of the skin from a mountain lion's tail. The arrows were kept in a foxskin quiver with the head down and the tail left on. It was hung on the Indian's back by a loop made of the skin of the hind legs. When the bow and arrows were not in use, they were hung on forked sticks high up in the Indian house.

I remember that sometimes white settlers or cattlemen would come to camp. They would always want to take down every bow they saw and string it and shoot it. They were always clumsy at it, and would damage the arrows and sometimes break the bow. But that was not the real reason the Indians were touchy about having their weapons handled.

The Indians shot most of their game from a distance of less than fifty feet. If possible, an Indian hunter would shoot deer at a range of twenty to thirty feet. He seldom fired an arrow that did not hit the deer in a vital place.

No white hunter could get that close to a deer, because the deer would scent him. Few white people knew how the Indian was able to get that close. Before going on a deer hunt, the Indian went into the sweat house and sweated for an hour, wearing his breechcloth. Then he ran and jumped into the water and washed himself off thoroughly. For several hours after such a bath, an Indian had no scent that a deer could smell. Now, there was no use in the Indian's going to all that trouble if his bow and arrows were going to carry the scent of a man. So he did not touch them until after he had come from his bath. No Indian would think of handling his weapons until he was ready to go hunting, and then only after he had sweated in the sweat house and bathed.

The Indians knew that smoke would kill the scent of a hunter. So, if one of them wanted to go hunting in a hurry, he would throw some weeds in the fire pit and stand in the smoke and turn round and round in it for a few minutes before he took down his bow and arrows. The effect of this was only good for about an hour and was of very little use in hunting deer, because deer were almost as afraid of fire and smoke as they were of a man.

Of course, the Indians knew dozens of things about the habits and likes and dislikes of deer that newcomers never even suspected. They also watched the direction of the wind very closely, and could call to them almost any game bird or animal in the hills.

When I was quite young, the Indians used to kill many deer by stalking and shooting them with the bow and arrow. For this sort of hunting, they prepared the horns and hide of the deer and placed them over themselves. The head of the deer was hollowed out and was fitted over the head of the hunter. The skin covered the back of the hunter. A short stick was carried in the right hand and was used to imitate the forelegs of a deer when the hunter bent forward. The bow and arrows were carried in the left hand. He would imitate a deer feeding and rubbing his horns on the brush, and many other actions of the deer, until he approached quite close to the game. Sometimes the hunter would work an hour to get just ten feet closer to the deer.

Hoey
(Deer)

The Indians also killed a good many deer by surrounding them. A hundred or more Indians would surround a deer in a thicket. Then two or three men with bows and arrows would go into the thicket. The Indians on the outside would yell and beat the brush and make enough noise to be heard two or three miles. The deer would be so badly scared that it didn't know which way to run. Finally, one of the men with a bow and arrows would get a shot at close range and kill the deer.

Deer and other large game were generally butchered in the field where they were killed. The people who killed the game generally carried it in and hung it in a tree in camp. Then the women took charge of it. I never saw a woman carry a deer.

The Indians I lived with used arrows tipped with obsidian and also arrows tipped with hardwood. They made a two-piece arrow, which had a shaft fitted with a socket in its fore-end, so that new points could be put on it. (They also made a one-piece arrow for use in practicing.) A good, straight arrow shaft was of more value to them than a point. By making the arrow of two pieces, they could remove a damaged point and place a good one on the shaft in a few seconds. In this way, there was no need to carry more than three or four shafts, rolled in moss and buckskin.

When game was shot with an arrow, the foreshaft and the point remained in the flesh, even though the animal might rub against the tules or brush and pull off the shaft. This was also an advantage in warfare, as the arrow could not be entirely removed without leaving a bad wound. If an arrow missed the game and the point was damaged by striking a rock, the shaft could be fitted with a new foreshaft and point and was ready for use immediately.

Obsidian-tipped arrows were used in warfare and in killing large game. For small game, the wooden-tipped arrows were used. Birds were killed with an arrow fitted with four crossed sticks near the tip.

The length of the arrow was determined by measuring the distance from the tip of the second finger of the hunter, arm extended to the side, to the opposite shoulder. I believe that the arrows were generally longer than would be used by a modern archer. War arrows were made of new-growth buttonwillow. This they would cut and scrape, using only the heartwood.

The making of arrow points of stone was practiced by some. I have seen hundreds of obsidian points chipped out. A piece of horn or bone was used to push, or pry, the flakes from the piece of obsidian. Sometimes blows were struck in the work, but I do not know how or why. It was only a matter of a few minutes to chip out an obsidian point.

The rear of the arrow shaft was fitted with three feathers. These were about five or six inches long. They were tied at the ends, but were left loose along the middle. Each man had a mark of his own on his arrows, so that he could prove that he had hit the game and that it had not been killed by someone else. The mark was also of value in proving ownership of arrows recovered after being lost.

In addition to small game, elk and deer were occasionally snared. The Choinumne also used to snare wild pigeons from a blind on

Kings River above Sycamore Creek. I have seen two Indians come in with at least a hundred pigeons apiece, snared in less than two hours. I heard one old Indian say that he alone had caught more than two hundred pigeons in one morning.

Snaring was done while the pigeons were drinking. They liked to drink at a spring or waterhole near tall trees, especially pines. They seldom drank at the main river, and they all tried to drink at the same hole. In the morning, about an hour after sunup, they would come to drink in flocks and droves, many thousands of them. They would light in such numbers that sometimes they would strip the limbs from the trees. It would take these large flocks from one to three hours to drink. When they left a waterhole, it was as badly drained and trampled as though a thousand sheep had drunk there.

Pigeon hunters built a blind close to the waterhole. It was a very clever arrangement. First, a smooth platform was leveled off as close to the water as possible. Then a shallow pit was dug on the side of the platform away from the water. It was large enough to hold two men lying down. The Indians I knew often hunted in pairs. This shallow pit was covered over with a light framework of bent limbs. Brush was put on the framework so the whole thing would look like a natural growth of brush.

On the side of the brush next to the level platform was a wide opening about eighteen inches high. A curtain of grass was hung across the opening. Near the middle of the platform, and about three feet from the grass curtain, was laid a pole about six feet long and three inches in diameter. To a pigeon the whole affair was the most harmless-looking thing possible.

Each pigeon hunter had several interesting pieces of equipment. First were two long snares. They were made of straight elderberry branches about eight feet long. On the tip of the branch was fastened a running noose, made of twisted, springy hair. It was formed by lashing a hair string about sixteen inches long to the stick. On the loose end of the string was fastened a stiff ring about an inch in diameter. This ring was slipped back on the stick to form a "u" shaped loop, the open side of the "u" closed by the stick. The loop was about six inches in diameter.

The hunters each had a captive pigeon in a cage made of cottonwood or willow twigs. The cage was about three feet long, a foot in diameter, and pointed at each end. Each also had a large bag of netting made from milkweed fiber.

About daylight, the hunters spread some ground acorn bait on the platform and then crawled through the brush into the rear of the pit. It was dark in there, and the pigeons could not see the hunters through the grass curtain across the front.

Each hunter took out his captive pigeon and blindfolded it. Then he tied one of its legs to a stick about an inch in diameter and five or six feet long, using a piece of string a foot long. When a pigeon is blindfolded, his feet grip onto whatever they touch like two vises. The Indians stood their pigeons on the end of the stick, and then poked them out through the curtain and rested the snare on the stick lying crossways on the platform outside. The pigeon teetered on his perch and sometimes flapped his wings in order to keep his balance.

The wild pigeons came in flights that would sometimes shut out the sun like a cloud. They piled into the nearest trees until there was

not a single place for another pigeon to sit. They were always wary of the water. No pigeon seemed to want to be the first to drink. In order to start them coming down, the hunters would pick up the sticks holding their decoys and move them around in the air. This made the decoys flap their wings in order to keep their balance. Immediately some of the wild pigeons decided all was safe and flew down to the platform. They saw the acorn crumbs and began eating. You understand, the pigeons were filling up on water before an all-day trip to their favorite wild rice or acorn feeding grounds, and were as hungry as they could get.

The hunters slowly slid their long snares out until a pigeon began picking up acorn meal from within the loop. The stick was then given a quick twist and a pull. The loop flipped up around the pigeon's neck and before he knew anything had happened he was flapping about and headed for the grass curtain.

By the time a pigeon had been snared, the platform was crowded with jumping, flapping, hungry pigeons, so the captured bird did not disturb the rest. Sometimes, in jerking a pigeon, two or more others would be knocked down. But they scarcely stopped eating. I have often seen two pigeons caught at the same time in one snare, and several times have seen three pulled in at once.

As soon as the hunter pulled the pigeon inside the curtain with one hand, he ran out a second loop with the other hand. He never took his eyes off the pigeons outside. He caught the captured pigeon between his knees, took off the loop, broke its neck with his thumb and forefinger, stuck it in the net, put the mouth of the net under his knee, and snaked in another pigeon with the other hand.

I helped snare pigeons twice, so I know just how it was done. It is about the only bird hunting I ever did. The old Indian I snared with could take in six or more pigeons while I was taking in one. But it was sure great sport.

We children used to snare rabbits on the plains, and sometimes squirrels and the little prairie foxes. The snares were made of bent withes and looped milkweed string.

Chapter Fourteen

Trip to Tulare Lake

FTER I HAD BEEN with the Indians periodically for several months, the time came for them to make one of their annual pilgrimages to Tulare Lake. It was their habit to go there yearly. The lakeshore was held by the Tache tribe, but the Choinumne were quite friendly with the Taches, and they made no objection to our using the lakeshore.

A great, long tule raft was built. They used to build small tule rafts that would carry one or two persons for use on Kings River below the rancheria opposite Sycamore Creek, but this raft for the lake trip was at least fifty feet long. It was made up of three long bundles of tules, pointed at each end, and bound together with willow withes.

The three bundles were made separately and then bound, or lashed, together with one at the bottom and two above, making a sort of keeled boat with a depression along the center of the deck. The tules were lashed together in such a way that the raft was pointed at the ends and resembled a great cigar, except that the pointed ends were turned up so that they were two or three feet above the deck.

Along the center of this raft was piled their supplies and camp equipment, including mortars and pestles, baskets of acorns, acorn bread, seeds, meat, skins for bedding, and many other things. On the sides of the boat sat eight or ten Indians, generally one or two families.

This raft that we used was not built to exclude water like a boat does [tule reeds float, but some water enters through the sides and floor of the boat]. On the lake, and sometimes in sloughs along the river, the tules used to float about loose. The wind would drift them into great mats near the shore. The fish used to collect under these mats and we used to walk over them and spear fish from them. I believe the Indians got their idea for the rafts from these great mats of floating tules. I remember that once we children bundled some of these floating tules together and used them as a boat.

For us children, the trip to Tulare Lake was an occasion of great excitement. We were all eyes and ears and could scarcely contain ourselves.

The trip was made in the late spring when the flood from the melting snows in the mountains provided enough water in the river to float the raft over the sandbars. The whole rancheria did not make the trip.

As I recollect, three rafts were built the first year. They were built several miles below Sycamore Creek, just how far I cannot say. We were almost a day carrying supplies from Sycamore down to the place where the rafts were built. It could have been ten miles below the rancheria. I do remember that the river was wide there, and that

great quantities of tules grew in a slough leading out from the river. It was in this slough that the raft had been built.

When we were all aboard, the boats were poled out into the stream and allowed to drift with the current. Three or four of the men stood at the sides of the raft and kept it away from snags and in the main current. In this way we floated along at about two or three miles an hour.

At night the raft was moored to the bank in a quiet place and we camped on the shore. It was really one of the greatest experiences I have ever had, and certainly the greatest I had while living with the Indians. I believe that they, too, enjoyed these trips more than any of their other experiences. We traveled in style and in comfort. The river was lined with trees and wild blackberry and grape vines, and the whole trip was one beautiful scene after another. In after years I used to cross Kings River many times on the bridge south of Kingsburg, and the scene there always reminded me of our trips.

We traveled very slowly and hunted a great deal along the way. Sometimes the hunters did not board the boat at all during the day, but met us with game when we had made camp in the evening. I suppose that it must have taken us at least ten days to go from Sycamore Creek to Tulare Lake.

Occasionally we met or saw Indians from other tribes along the river. They were all friendly and seemed to take our trip as a matter of course. I remember that once a party of three of these Indians rode with us all day.

At the lake we made a permanent camp on some high ground along a slough. I believe that they had used this place before, as one of the women dug up a mortar and pestle that had been buried there previously.

We found the lake Indians near us living in some ways quite differently from the Indians at Sycamore Creek. They talked enough of our language that we could understand them readily, but the rest of their life differed.

The houses at the lake were the thing I noticed most. I do not remember having seen a house there like those upstream. Generally they were built of thin tule mats and were quite long—some of them were at least one hundred feet long. A sort of wooden ridge was erected on crotched poles set in the ground, and the tule mats were leaned up against it. Everything else was of a more temporary nature than I was used to at Sycamore Creek.

The shorelines of Tulare Lake changed and shifted a great deal. If a strong wind came from the north, as it often did, the water would move several miles south, and would move again when the wind

Tulare Lake house

changed. Then, when the water level in the lake changed, both the lea and windward shorelines shifted long distances. At some point it was possible to wade out into the lake as far as a mile and find the water below our knees. This made it impossible for the Indians to stay in one place permanently and they could roll up their light houses and load them on tule rafts and move in a few hours.

While we were at the lake I noticed one or two houses that have ever since been more or less of a puzzle to me. They were built in the standing tules, and seemed to be woven from the living tules as they stood in place. They were dome-shaped and about ten feet in diameter. I never saw any more of them and I have never since met anyone who had seen one of them. As I remember them, the tules appeared to have been cut away inside the house, but no excavation had been made as was made for the willow houses upstream.

The tule mats that I have mentioned were made in two ways. Some were tied together with tule by a series of half hitches. The tules were laid out on the ground parallel to each other and close together. Then about every foot or so they were tied together by cross tules and the half hitches.

Other mats were laid out in the same way, and a milkweed string was passed through them. Holes were punched in the tules by means of a bone awl, and the string was run through the holes. These mats were used for floor coverings and mattresses, as I have mentioned, and for many other purposes. At the lake a light framework of driftwood was set up and the tule mats laid over it to provide a shade. This shade was used in other places, but was generally covered with brush instead of tule mats.

The milkweed string was made of a tall milkweed that grew on the plains and foothills. It was a velvety, bluish-green weed, consisting principally of a straight stalk from three to four feet in height. Along the stalk were leaves, and at the top was a blossom which later developed into seed pods.

On the outside of the woody center was a covering of fiber considerably like flax. During the winter this loose fiber was gathered after it had fallen from the dead stalks to the ground and was used in making string. The string was twisted by means of a small stick rolled on the thigh.

When twisted, the string had much the appearance of the common sack twine used for sewing grain bags. The milkweed string was used for an almost unlimited number of purposes.

The Indians who lived on the river below Centerville also made string from the fiber of a kind of wild hemp, a tall, straight-stalked plant with red bark. They pounded the stalks between two rocks and removed the fiber with their fingers. It made a red string and was as strong as that made from milkweed.

From the sap of the same milkweed used for making the string a sort of chewing gum was made. This was obtained in a rather peculiar way. The green milkweed stalk was cut. The milk immediately began to form in a large drop on the cut end. This end was dabbed on a clay ball. This was repeated as often as a drop of milk would form on the cut end. Then another cut was made, and the process was repeated. The milk dried on the clay ball in a sort of gummy coating. This coating was peeled off and chewed. It was about the same as ordinary chewing gum after the sugar has been dissolved from it in chewing.

For fishing and hunting on the lake, a tule raft was used. This raft was constructed in a different way from the one I have already described. It was wide and flat and would pass over very shallow water. It was pointed at the ends, but the points were not raised as high as they were on the raft used on the river.

In the center of the fishing raft was a large hole. Through this hole fish were gigged much as they were from the platform on the river. The fisherman lay on his stomach with his head and shoulders over this hole, which was covered with a tule mat so he could see into the water without being seen by the fish

A few feet ahead of the hole was an earthen, or mud, hearth. On this hearth a fire was kindled, and the cooking was done.

Sometimes three or four Indians would go out on the lake on one of the fishing rafts and hunt ducks and geese and stay out there as long as a week. During this time they poled the raft around through the tules and ate and slept on it.

They would throw loose tules over the raft and themselves, forming a blind. Then, through the hole in the center they would slowly pole the raft wherever they wanted to go. In this way they would approach within a few feet of ducks and geese and shoot them from the blind with bows and arrows.

Sometimes they would catch the ducks that flew overhead in a net. This net was a good deal like the net fishermen use to take trout out of the water after they have hooked them. It was about two feet across at the mouth. They also snared ducks and geese among the tules.

The Indians could imitate the call of almost any animal or bird, and they used to make use of this in hunting. They commonly called ducks, geese, rabbits, and deer.

The tribe I was with had an interesting way of catching fish on the lake shore. A weir [dam] of willow wickerwork was built out at an angle from the shore for a distance of fifty or sixty yards. Then a large group of Indians would wade out beyond the weir. This group would form a semicircle sometimes a mile long.

After the circle was completed they would close in, all splashing and yelling and driving the fish into the shallow water behind the weir. In this shallow water were two or three Indians wading about, each with one of the bottomless wicker baskets that they used up the river for catching fish in pools. When they felt a fish with their feet or saw a ripple made by a fish, they would clap the basket down and catch it. It was not possible to see the fish as the shallow water soon became very muddy.

One of the great sports at the lake was the jackrabbit drive. The flat sagebrush plains around the lake were fairly alive with jackrabbits, and the Indians used to plan a drive much like the drives later made by the white people, except that they used no pen or corral.

A milkweed string net was made. This was about thirty feet long and four feet high. It was tied just like an ordinary fish seine [net], but I never saw the Indians seine fish. This net was used only for catching rabbits. The net was erected between two large sage bushes. Then a long line of Indians marched out at an angle from each end of it. Most of these Indians carried a stick about two feet long. When the two lines of Indians had formed wings several hundred yards long the outer ends closed in and then they drove the enclosed rabbits toward the net.

When an Indian came close enough to a rabbit he would throw his stick spinning at it and would generally break its legs. But most of the rabbits were killed at the net. As the rabbits ran along between the two lines of Indians they saw what they thought was an opening in the line at the net. They attempted to run through this opening, but hit the net and bounced back. Then they were promptly clubbed by one of two or three Indians who were hiding there for that purpose.

It surely was exciting when the drivers had closed in. There would be hundreds of rabbits and almost as many sticks flying in the air. Many of the rabbits would break through the line of Indians and escape, but a great many, probably two hundred, would be killed in a forenoon [morning] drive.

The skins were taken from the rabbits without being split, and while green they were cut into long strips about three-quarters of an inch wide. As the strips dried, they naturally curled up with the flesh side inside and the fur on the outside. This made a sort of fur boa about an inch and a half in diameter.

The rabbitskins were made into fine blankets. These were used as a covering for sleeping, much like an ordinary blanket. They were the warmest and most comfortable bed covering I have ever used.

In making the blanket, two of the strings were twisted together for a distance of about six feet. Then the ends were doubled back and looped through the twists of the first portion. Working back and forth across the blanket in this way it was woven into a square about six feet on each side.

Smaller blankets were used as a sort of cape, or shawl, in extremely cold weather, or to wrap the babies in before they were strapped on the cradle. The women also made their skirts in this way.

We used to see elk and antelope around the lake. I heard about the Indians surrounding antelope, but I never saw it done. They used to shoot both elk and antelope from blinds when they came to the lake to water.

Antelope were easily killed with arrows, but elk were almost too much for them. It was almost impossible for them to kill an elk outright with their weapons. They would shoot arrows into an elk and then follow it for several days until it was weak enough to be overpowered.

Súey-all
(Antelope)

My brother Ben once killed an elk on Tulare Lake. When he was dressing it, he noticed an unnatural growth inside the body. Upon investigating, he found it to be the foreshaft of an arrow which had lodged there and had entirely healed over, both inside and outside.

We left the lake for the last time in the summer. We were all sorry to go. There was an almost unlimited amount of game there and always lots of excitement in hunting and fishing. The lake was a great attraction to the Indians, just as it later was to the white people.

We started back with our supplies piled on the raft and poled it as far up the river as the slack water extended. Then the women loaded our supplies on their backs and we trudged back to Sycamore Creek. The rafts were abandoned at the side of the river.

I am sure that we carried back none of the portable stone mortars and pestles that we had rafted down earlier in the summer. It is my belief that they were buried at the lake campsite for future use. When we arrived at the lake, one of the women dug up a mortar that she had buried there previously.

It probably took us longer to make the trip from the lake back to Sycamore Creek than it had taken to make the down trip. I remember that it was a long, hot journey and that we were weary when we arrived at the rancheria.

Following our arrival back at the rancheria, I was with the Indians almost continually until about 1857. After that I was with them most of the time, but I stayed with my daddy and my brothers when they were at home.

During this time I hunted and fished with the Indians and learned all about their way of living. By this time, the Indians were wearing old cast-off clothing, given to them by the white people. I dressed like my brothers, wearing the common work clothes of the day.

Chapter Fifteen

Problems Begin

I MADE TWO TRIPS to Tulare Lake with the Indians. If my memory is accurate, they were made in the summers of 1853 and 1854. I do not believe that my tribe made any such trips later than 1855, as the reservations had broken up their routine. They had been deprived of their game and were rapidly starved and crowded into the hills in competition with their hostile mountain neighbors. I never again saw one of the large tule rafts after the second trip.

One thing happened on our second trip to the lake that I will never forget. I had not seen my daddy for a year or more. He had been away with horses and cattle and hogs, in the mountains and on the plains, and I did not know where he was.

It was late in the forenoon of a hot, sultry, summer day. Several Indian boys and I were shooting with our bows and arrows at a dummy duck in the edge of the lake. We used to do this almost every day, and sometimes we would be lucky enough to get a shot at a fish. I saw a party of three horsemen passing at a distance of several hundred yards.

I watched the travelers until they passed us. Something about them was puzzling to me, and I finally saw that one of them was my daddy. I will never forget how lost and helpless I felt at the time. My heart seemed to sink down to my feet. I wanted to see him so badly, and I was sure I could not catch him. But I ran after him anyway, and called to him, hoping to attract his attention.

Of course he neither heard nor saw me. However, I kept on until I could go no farther and, after falling down several times and becoming hot and entirely out of breath and helpless, I lay in the tules, crying.

One of the Indians who was fishing about a quarter of a mile or more away, closer to where my daddy was passing, saw what was going on. He ran out from the lake and stopped them. Then they rode back to where I was. I was still lying in the tules, because I was ashamed to let the Indian boys see that I was crying, and was feeling about as homesick as I have ever felt. I did not know what had been done after I had fallen, and was about as surprised a boy as ever lived when my daddy rode up and took me on his horse.

My daddy had not expected to see me at the lake. He had left us at Sycamore Creek. But the Indians had made a trip to the lake in the meantime, and he had not known of it.

After my daddy took me on his horse, the Indians, who had been fishing nearby, collected and led him to their camp. He stayed with us about an hour and had dinner. Then he had to go to look after some cattle he was rounding up, and I did not see him again for about two years.

All of the Indians, even the children, were very serious about this experience of mine and never teased me, or made any reference to my crying, as I know they would have under any other circumstances. They were afraid that my daddy would take me away with him and were pleased when he left me. I was willing to stay with the Indians and did not ask him to take me with him.

At the time of our second trip to the lake, one other thing happened that I will never forget. The government had been trying to establish Indian reservations on Kings and Fresno Rivers and a troop of cavalry [soldiers on horseback] was attempting to round up all of the Indians in the valley. The Indians had been dying off rapidly in the few years previous to the establishment of the reservations and there were not many of them left. But even with the few Indians, it was almost impossible, as the Indians did not want to go on the reservation. I never blamed them for this, as it was simply a means of getting their land away from them and they knew it. They scattered and hid in the tules. All of our group at the lake escaped.

There was a white man by the name of Mann living near the lake with his Indian wife. They had been living there for several years. A squad of cavalry rode up to the door of the cabin one day and demanded the woman. Mann told them that she was his wife; that he had provided for her for several years, and that he could continue to do so in the future.

The leader of the squad told Mann to bring her out, and when Mann refused the leader knocked the door open and entered the cabin. The woman had crawled under the bed, and the cavalrymen started to drag her out. She called to Mann for help. Mann ran to her aid and was shot in the back and killed by one of the troopers outside.

The troopers tied the woman and took her with them and left Mann lying where he had fallen. The Indians I was with knew Mann and buried him after the squad of cavalry left. I did not see what happened, but some of the Indians of our party did. A short time afterward, we saw the woman who had been taken away when Mann was killed. I have many times heard her tell what happened.

I expect that this story about the killing of Mann sounds pretty bad and probably a number of other things I am telling about the Indians and the white people may give the impression that I favor the Indians and am prejudiced against the white people. In the first place, I have never talked about my life with the Indians because I had very little to tell that the white people liked to hear. I knew the Indians in their natural state and I know that they were the finest people that I have ever met. I am not telling what I would like to be able to tell; only what I heard and saw.

Chapter Sixteen

Conflict and Tragedy

After the reservation was formed and the white settlers began to come into the valley in great numbers, the Indians had a hard time of it. I used to hear all of their troubles discussed at the rancheria where I lived, and I know how they felt about the way they were treated.

The elk and antelope were all gone in just a few years. Fences were built and the Indians were not allowed to roam about and gather plants and seeds and hunt as they had done before. They were forced into contact with the Monaches and other mountain Indians. I believe that this had as much to do with their disappearance as anything else.

They were finally crowded into small camps and had to shear sheep and wash clothes for the white settlers about them. White men were always furnishing them liquor and many of them were killed by whiskey. Whiskey made devils of them. Quarrels and fights would take place between parties who had always been friends and when such quarrels arose, someone was sure to be badly knifed or shot. The older men of the tribe tried to stop them, but could do nothing with them.

The Indians were quite honest among themselves and never stole from one another. I believe they were more truthful among themselves than the white people.

The Indians thought that the white people were smarter and cleverer than they were and they looked to the whites many times for advice, until they found they could not trust them at all. They would do many things when advised to by the whites that they would not think of doing upon the advice of their own people. In their own life, marriage consisted simply of providing a home for the bride. Many white scamps would fix up a cabin for one of the Indian women and then when they wanted to would go away and leave her. She would provide for and raise the children. Many times she was better off when he did leave, as she otherwise had to provide for him also. The early settlers used to be scandalized when a white man married an Indian woman. I believe that in nine cases out of ten the Indian woman was the loser in the bargain and was better than the man she married.

Then, too, some of the Indians started living in houses. They could not stand an indoor life and many died of consumption [tuberculosis] and measles. When they had these diseases, they would go in the sweat house and sweat for an hour or more and then jump in the cold streams. This killed them by the hundreds.

They had never known about fevers. The sweat house was a good remedy for rheumatism, but it was deadly when used as a treatment for fevers.

When I left the Indians for the last time in 1862, there were not more than forty left, of a group that numbered more than three hundred when I went to them in 1850 or 1851. Battles with the whites accounted for very few of those missing, for the Choinumne I was with, as a group, had no battles with the whites. I believe that a few of the young men joined in some of the difficulties for the excitement they could get from it, but only a very few individuals.

After the trouble with the Indians, my daddy started running hogs on Tulare Lake. My daddy and Jack Gordon were in partnership. They took three Indians with them and went to San Luis Obispo. There they bought eight hundred head of white hogs. For just a few dollars they also bought a band of mustang horses. They drove the horses ahead of the hogs. The hogs were kept in good shape all the way to Tulare Lake.

My daddy was a great man for action. He always traveled light. He would start out on a trip over the San Joaquin plains without so much as a pack animal. He would put some bread and jerky in a sack, roll it up in a blanket, tie the blanket behind the saddle, fill a couple of large canteens with water and he was ready for a three weeks' trip.

My daddy and Gordon put their hogs on Tulare Lake to feed on tule roots and mussels. After the hogs had fattened at the lake, they were taken to the Sierra foothills. At that time of the year the acorns were ripe and they drove the hogs north through the acorn belt and sold them at the mines in Mariposa and Tuolumne counties. This venture proved to be quite profitable.

But Jack Gordon was a bandit. The hog business was merely a cover under which he carried on many crimes. My daddy suspected this for a long time and after he was sure about Gordon's activities outside of the hog business he found some excuse for dissolving the partnership. Gordon was clever in his dealings and was not generally suspected of any crooked work. Gordon was a dangerous man and would shoot to kill upon the slightest provocation.

By 1860 my daddy began staying around Visalia most of the time. He had taken up a piece of land near there and kept several good horses that he entered in the races at the track in Visalia.

When the Civil War broke out, conditions were bad in the Four Creeks country, where my daddy was staying. Almost everyone around there was a southerner and they had to establish a military post, called Camp Babbitt, to keep them in order—to keep Visalia from seceding from the Union, as some of the southerners around there used to say. My daddy was a southerner and his sympathies were with the South. But when it came to actually taking up arms against the Union, he could not do it. I guess he had been in the army too much to change to the Confederate army.

About this time, my daddy decided that I had been with the Indians long enough. So early in 1862, he took me over to Visalia and put me in school. When I started to school, I believe that my speech must have been a little peculiar from having talked so much Indian. It may have been that I unconsciously used a few Indian words. At least the boys at school used to make fun of me. I had to whip every boy in school before they would let me alone about it.

Then, too, there seemed at this time in the minds of many white people to be some sort of a stigma attached to my life with the Indians. I had considerable trouble over this while I was around Visalia and had to whip several persons because of it.

From then on I resolved to never speak of my life with the Indians. People in general had so many wrong notions about Indians and were so ignorant about their lives that I was continually drawn into arguments about them. Everyone was so sure they knew all about Indians that I made up my mind I would never tell them any different.

A Choinumne Glossary

áw-gáwish	sister
áw-push	moon
báh-pish	grandmother
bo-có-lah	a snoop
búh-so	a braggart
cáw-bush	embrace given in greeting
Chaw-láw-no	San Joaquin Valley
chi-úhk-nim	niece or nephew
chólo wé-chep	little white boy
chú-la-pee	six
drah-lip	bow
ha-nów-ish	Choinumne guessing game
he ahm	I am, you are, he is, she is, we are, they are
He ahm wih-níh-se	I am ready, you are ready, he/she is ready, we are ready, they are ready
hi-él	summer
hoey	deer
hói-up	blue lupine (a flower)
hóme-tun	blunted or dull point
hóp-poo-noy	four
Joul-bú-sho	I have something that I wish to share
k-hú-mote	south
k-hú-sheem	north
lúp-chen súh-suh	baby-blue eyes (a flower)
mah	you

min	yours
mo-hó-o	black bear
moó-nosh	eight
múh-loosh	a cheat
ná-bits	brother
nah	me
náw-hawn	grizzly bear
nih-súh-now	blunted or dull edge
nim	mine
nó-pope	father
nó-um	mother
núm-chen	seven
óo-push	sun
péek-ook	ground owl
peesh	imaginary beast
poó-noy	two
poo-noy shinto	two hundred
poo-noy treeo	twenty
poo-noy treeo poo-noy	twenty-two
poo-noy treeo ya-et	twenty-one
pów-putch	porcupine
shuh-cúg-cuh	California poppy
sím-sim	bat
skée-til	squirrel
só-pun-hut	nine
so-pun-hut shinto	nine hundred
só-uh-pun	three
so-uh-pun treeo	thirty
so-uh-pun treeo	
so-uh-pun	thirty-three
súey-all	antelope
swoop	hawk
t-hú-k-héel	west

Ta-míd-um	Where are your manners?
tah-lúh-wush	Choinumne game, similar to football
taw-máw-kish	winter
tish-úm-yu	spring; time when wildflowers bloom
To-trá shee-uh	That is bad business
to-tree	bad
too-yosh	arrow
tow-so tow-so	one million
trá-el-le en-él-o	Chinese house (a flower)
tréeo	ten
treeo poo-noy	twelve
treeo so-uh-pun	thirteen
treeo treeo	one hundred
treeo ya-et	eleven
tríp-nee	supernatural
trúh-now	badger
wá-tih-te	alternate name for ground owl
wah-áh-hah bah-lu Chaw-láw-no	Away down the San Joaquin Valley
Wah-áh-hah tríp-in	I have been for a long trip
Wah tríp-in	I have been for a short trip
wáts-wats	duck
wáwh-yen	sleep
wé-che	very small
wé-chep	small child
wé-chet	small sticks
wé-ghe	small
we-há-set	mountain lion
yách-chee-nil	five
yach-chee-nil treeo	fifty
yá-et	one
ya-et shinto	one hundred
ya-et tów-so	one thousand

Thomas Jefferson Mayfield at age 84 in 1928